Lion Adventure

A Willard Price Adventure Story, about Hal
and Roger and their amazing adventures in
search of wild animals for the world's zoos.

Hal and Roger are in East Africa hunting
man-eating lions. Their job is to protect the
railway workers from the lions which, once
they have tasted human flesh, prefer it to
anything else. But someone seems anxious to
get rid of the two boys, as they discover to their
cost when they find themselves adrift in their
observation balloon, without food and water,
and being carried swiftly towards dangerous,
inhospitable mountains. A nasty crash-landing
nearly finishes them, but, surprisingly, it is the
lions which eventually help save their lives.

Willard Price

Lion adventure

Illustrated by Pat Marriott

KNIGHT BOOKS
Hodder & Stoughton

Note

*The characters in this story are fictional
with the exception of Michael Grzimek,
Dr Louis Leaky, and Joy Adamson. The
descriptions of the habits of animals and
customs of the people are factual.
The Emperor Haile Selassie, mentioned
on page 90, was deposed in 1974.
He died in 1975.*

Text © 1967 by Willard Price
Illustrations © 1967 by Jonathan Cape Ltd

First published 1967 by Jonathan Cape Ltd

This edition first published 1970 by Knight Books

Twelfth impression 1983

Printed and bound in Great Britain for
Hodder and Stoughton Paperbacks, a
division of Hodder and Stoughton Ltd.,
Mill Road, Dunton Green, Sevenoaks,
Kent (Editorial Office: 47 Bedford
Square, London, WC1 3DP) by
Richard Clay (The Chaucer Press), Ltd., Bungay, Suffolk

ISBN 0 340 10435 X

Contents

1

Man-eater wanted

It seemed a wild thing to do – lie out in lion country waiting to be attacked by a man-eater.

But Hal was not wild. He was a steady nineteen-year-old, six feet tall, with the strength and brains of a man. He had thought it over carefully. This had seemed the best way to go at it.

His brother, thirteen-year-old Roger, agreed – not because he was a heavy thinker – he wasn't – but it sounded like an exciting adventure.

So now they lay on the ground within a circle of piled-up thorn bushes. In Africa they call it a *boma*. It is supposed to protect you against wild beasts. Roger didn't feel very well protected.

'It's only five feet high,' he whispered. 'A lion could easily jump over it.'

'But he won't,' replied Hal. 'Not unless he's a real man-eater. Most lions leave you alone, provided you leave them alone.'

'Then why have a boma at all? Why not just sit out in the open?'

'You'd be inviting trouble if you did that. Suppose a lion or leopard or rhino or elephant or most any animal stumbled on you in the dark. He'd be surprised. He'd probably take a swipe at you in self-defence. One swipe would be enough. But all animals hate thorns. If they touch this boma they'll veer off. At least, I hope they will.'

'Except a man-eater.'

'Yes, except a man-eater. We've got the welcome mat out for him. If he gets our scent he's pretty sure to pay us a visit.'

'And you'd like that,' Roger said with a sort of shiver in his voice.

'Sure I'd like that. That's what we're here for. What's the matter, kid? Scared?'

'Not on your life,' protested Roger. 'Just cold.'

Hal and Roger had come to Africa, not to kill animals but to take them alive. They had been trained by their father, John Hunt, famous animal collector, in the difficult art of capturing living animals and shipping them to zoos and circuses. But tonight their job was not to save animals but to get rid of them.

It had been a strange day. It began with five murders. Five men repairing tracks on the Nairobi–Mombasa railway near the village of Tsavo were killed and eaten by lions.

The lions of the Tsavo region had always had a bad reputation. Years ago when the railway was first being laid, newspapers the world over told the grim story of 'the man-eaters of Tsavo' who were killing and devouring railway workers by the score. Now these lions or their descendants were at it again.

The boys, already well known for their success in taking animals, were asked to help find the killers. This was no easy job. How were they to know which lions were man-eaters and which were innocent? The innocent must be saved, for they are one of the great sights of Africa. Visitors come from all over the world to see the African lions. Africa is their last home. Long ago there were lions in many lands – Europe, Arabia, Palestine, India ... As men multiplied, lions were killed off, and now Africa is the last stand of the 'King of Beasts'. It would be a pity to let this most majestic of animals become extinct.

But how save the good lions and yet get rid of the bad actors? You could not simply go out with a gun and kill all lions. You must have a way of discovering which were man-eaters and which were not.

Hal had found a way. He would offer the lions two kinds of bait: one was animal, the other human. The animal was a dead goat and it lay in the clearing ten yards in front of the boma. The human bait was the boys themselves.

An approaching lion could smell both the goat and the boys. If it preferred to eat the goat it was not a man-eater. But if it turned up its nose at the goat and attacked the boma it was a man-eater.

Roger didn't like the idea of being set out as dinner for a lion.

'Besides, it won't work,' he said. 'Suppose the lion eats the goat. That doesn't prove he isn't a man-eater.'

'Yes it does,' insisted Hal. 'A real man-eater won't touch an animal so long as it has a chance to eat human flesh.'

'Why? Are we so delicious?'

'The lion thinks so. Once he has dined on a human

he's not satisfied with animal meat. Scientists say the reason is that human flesh is salty. And tender. A man's muscles are soft compared with those of an antelope that has to keep jumping all day every day to make a living. And Man's hide is not tough. And there is no fur or feathers or sharp quills to get stuck in His Majesty's jaws. Anyhow, there's no danger. We have our thirty safari men to protect us.'

It hadn't quite worked out that way. When Tanga, the station master who had reported the death of five workers, took the boys to the Tsavo district officer, that black giant said sourly:

'No. No thirty men. Just you two.'

'But how can we do the job alone?'

'That's your problem. No men.'

'Would you give us a reason?'

The officer glared. 'Why should I give you a reason? I was a chief, and my father and grandfather were chiefs. My people called me King Ku. I am still King Ku. A king gives no reasons.'

'You are not a king,' Hal reminded him. 'You are a district officer responsible to the people of Kenya.'

King Ku leaped to his feet. 'Pig! I should have you flogged. You whites should remember that Kenya is a black man's country now. We owe no reasons to whites.' He waved his fly-whisk, symbol of a chief's authority. 'All right, I'll give you a reason. Your crew would kill many lions, bad ones and good ones. We can't have that. So you must act alone.'

Hal said no more. Later he said to Roger, 'I wonder what his real reason is. Why is he so down on whites? Almost seems as if he wants to get us killed.'

2

The innocents

THERE was a scraping sound in the bushes.

'Listen. Perhaps that's His Nibs.'

Hal took up his Lee Enfield ·303. It was a good gun for a lion hunt. It had a ten-cartridge magazine. And there was another cartridge in the chamber. Eleven shots. It just could take that many to kill a lion.

Hal had not allowed his brother to bring a gun. The kid might not know how to handle it. Besides, someone had to hold the electric torch and throw its spotlight on the lion. That was Roger's job.

But Roger was not entirely unarmed. Beside him lay a ten-foot spear. One of his men had urged him to take it along. The man was a Masai, and the Masai are famous for their skill in killing a lion with nothing but a spear. Roger's Masai friend had taught him how to use it.

Hal thought it was all nonsense. A Masai warrior might kill with a spear. But it was foolish for his kid brother to think he could do anything with it. Oh well, it would do no harm to let him bring it along.

Roger had also brought a thunderflash. It could be thrown at a beast and would explode in his face and was supposed to scare him out of his wits.

'Light up,' whispered Hal.

Roger turned on his torch. A dozen animals were tug-

ging at the goat. What a disappointment – they were not
lions but those homely humpbacks, the hyenas.

They paid no attention to the light but kept tugging at
the carcass. They began to drag it off towards the
bushes. If they got away with that, it would spoil the
whole plan.

'Take a crack at them,' Roger urged. 'Scare them
away.'

'And scare off the lions too? No – we've got to keep
quiet.'

'But we can't let them spoil everything. How about
stones?'

'Okay, if we can find some.' He explored the ground
with his hand. 'Here's one.'

Hal stood up and hurled the stone. It smacked a
hyena on the jowl and brought forth an unearthly
scream.

But it did not scare off the hyenas. Instead, they raised
their heads from their dinner and started sniffing about
for their enemy. Then they came snarling and sneaking
through the grass towards the boma.

The hyena is said to be a coward. Those who say it do

not know the beast. True, a lone hyena will not attack a man unless the man is asleep. Then the beast will not hesitate to slip under the tent flaps and bite off a foot or a face. Many a hunter has been disfigured for life by a single hyena. But a man awake and alert will not be touched, if the hyena is alone.

If the hyena is one of a pack it is quite a different matter. Knowing that his companions will help him, he becomes bold and savage. So now the boys were completely surrounded by big-jawed bone-crushers seeking a hole large enough to admit their slinking bodies.

Roger kept circling the light along the inside of the thorn wall, watching for the first nose to come through. When it did, Hal whacked it with the butt of his gun and the nose withdrew, leaving nothing but a hole and a howl.

But another nose pushed through, enlarging the hole. Another whack. A growl on the other side signalled the breaking through of another hole. Then another.

It was impossible to look in all directions at once and punish every impertinent nose. In a few minutes the pack would be inside the boma.

The boys were saved by the very sort of animal they had come to hunt. A deep roar made Roger turn his light outside the boma. There was a huge lion, who had heard the hyenas scream, and had come to investigate. The hyenas had a sudden change of mind. They left the boma and ran yelping into the underbrush.

The lion approached the boma. Hal levelled his gun. 'Keep the light on him,' he said. This was a poor bargain, Hal thought. They had traded a pack of hyenas for something more dangerous.

The light danced on the lion's face – Roger's torch hand was wobbling.

'Keep that thing steady,' said Hal.

'Pot him,' Roger urged.

But Hal did not fire.

The lion stopped, staring into the light. It was not afraid, only fascinated. Lions are like humans – all different. Some fear light, some do not. Lions have been known not only to approach a campfire, but to lie down in the hot ashes to get warm.

The eyes of the beast, twice as large as man's, shone like golden lanterns. It is the presence of a mirror in a cat's eye that accounts for the glow whenever a strong light is played upon the eyes at night. Roger found something terrifying in those blazing eyes.

'Shoot, you dope. What's stopping you?'

Hal still waited, finger on trigger.

The big beast was sniffing. A breeze carried the boys' scent straight up those wide nostrils. The lion stood still, within five feet, an absolutely perfect shot.

Hal was tempted to pull the trigger. This animal might or might not be a man-eater, but he was too close for comfort. Why take a chance? It was better to slaughter the wrong animal than to take the risk of being slaughtered.

But still he waited, and the light danced. The lion put up his head as if he smelled something that did not please him. He turned slowly and went back to the dead goat. He began to feed.

Hal put down his gun and relaxed. He felt as if he had been bound hand and foot and his blood had stopped circulating. He put his arm around his younger brother.

The boy was trembling, but refused to admit that he had been scared. 'Sure is cold, isn't it?' said Roger.

'Sure is.'

Anyhow it was true. The night air of mile-high East Africa becomes surprisingly chilly no matter how hot the day.

The lion raised his great bushy head and looked off into the brush. Then he made a most peculiar sound. It was not a roar. It was a soft, penetrating *um-um-um-um*.

'Calling his mate,' Hal whispered.

Hal knew lion talk pretty well. He was already a trained naturalist. He had dealt with animals all his nineteen years on his father's animal farm and in the world. He knew that lions make a greater variety of sounds than almost any other animal, and every sound means something.

A deep muffled *ugh-ugh-ugh* means that the lion is looking for food. A charging lion is apt to give off a series of deep coughing grunts. A lion usually does not roar before he has eaten – that would scare away all the game. After his dinner he roars – and what a roar it is! It can be heard for many miles. It reaches much farther than even the scream of an elephant. It means something like, 'I have come and killed and eaten – I am a great fellow.'

Two lions walking along together will indulge in almost constant conversation. It consists of sighs, low grunts, wheezing noises, snoring sounds, moans, deep rumblings like those that come from the low notes of an organ.

When a lioness is talking to her cubs she sounds very

much like a human mother, using soft, gentle, comforting baby talk. The cubs reply with plaintive little miaows that sound almost exactly like those of a house cat.

But this lion's mate replied with none of these sounds. She answered him with a low whistle. It sounded quite like the note of a sleepy bird. Who would imagine that a lion could whistle? The sound could deceive a human and would not alarm game.

A big tawny lioness came padding out of the bushes in the light of Roger's torch. The lion stepped aside to let her share his dinner. A lion is not like a hyena. The hyena never wants to share anything with anybody, even his wife. The lion is a family man. He eats first – but he doesn't forget his mate and his cubs.

But the lioness, approaching the goat, suddenly stopped and stared at the boma. She stretched her head towards it and sniffed strongly. The boys wished at that moment that they were not so smellable.

She lowered herself to a crouching position and crept towards the wall of thorns. Roger's light wobbled, and even Hal felt a sudden chill crawling up his backbone. He brought his gun to his shoulder.

3

The twisted gun

THE lioness came straight up to the boma, asking questions with her nose.

She raised her paw and gave the wall a light swat. The whole structure shivered. If she swatted again, a little harder, it would fall down. But she evidently didn't like the feel of the thorns. She started on a circuit of the boma and Roger followed her with his light.

'I'd shoot if I were you,' he whispered to Hal.

'Perhaps she's just curious,' replied Hal, knowing that lady lions were much like lady humans.

Having completed the circle, the lioness stood on her hind feet, put her front paws on the top of the wall, and looked inside. Roger put his hand on his spear.

'Steady,' whispered Hal. 'Don't move.'

For ten seconds that seemed like ten minutes the lioness looked. Then she gave a snort as if expelling a bad odour from her nose, dropped to the ground, and padded out to join her husband at dinner.

Hal lowered his gun. She had passed the test with flying colours – she was no man-eater.

One goat was not enough food for two big animals. And yet it was not in lion nature to be selfish. When the male and his mate had partially satisfied their own hunger, they stood back. The lion raised his head to the skies and let out his thunderous after-dinner roar. That notified all lions within miles that dinner was being served.

In a matter of minutes they began emerging from the brush. Eight lions made short work of what was left of the goat.

But there was a ninth lion that did not take part. He looked different from the others – evidently not a member of the same 'pride' or related group. He was older, bigger, bore a heavy mane that was black instead of the usual light brown, and he sat alone, staring straight into the light from the boma.

Though he would have nothing to do with the goat he was apparently hungry, for moisture kept dripping from the corners of his mouth. Presently he rose and came slowly towards the boma.

'Here we go again,' said Hal, a little wearily.

The boys were getting used to it. They could not remain scared every time a lion came sniffing around. Probably this one would behave like the others. He would be disgusted with the man-smell and would go back to the goat.

It was at this moment that Roger began to itch.

'Something's biting me,' he said.

'Probably just nervousness,' said Hal.

Then he felt it himself. A crawling over his skin and a nipping at the most tender parts.

'Ants!' he exclaimed.

Why couldn't they have waited until this lion hunt was over?

The ground had been carefully examined for ant-nests before the boma was built. These were evidently army ants, coming from heaven knows where, marching in a column like a well-trained army, eating up everything on the way. They had chosen to parade straight through the boma.

'Let's get out of here,' said Roger, standing up and trying to shake the pests out of his clothes.

'You stay right here and keep quiet,' Hal ordered.

'Keep quiet! How can you keep quiet when you're being eaten alive?'

'Better the ants than the lions.'

'Oh, I'm not afraid of him. He'll be just like the others. Give us the once-over and then leave us flat.'

'I don't know,' said Hal. 'He acts as if he meant business.'

The lion's tail was twitching back and forth. Then it stood up straight and stiff like the mast of a ship. The ears were laid back. The teeth were bared. There was no roaring – just a soft *ughing*.

At this angle Hal could not use a heart shot. He must hit the brain. The brain was not up there in the top of the head – he knew that. That was all hair and nothing else. To get the brain he must strike between the eyes. He aimed his gun accordingly.

The lion flattened himself on the ground. This was called the 'spread'. After the spread comes the spring.

The ants were biting. Hal tried to ignore them. As the lion's claws bit into the earth, Hal fired. At the same instant Roger hurled the thunderflash. It struck the ground directly in front of the lion's nose and exploded. The lion gave it a contemptuous swat with his paw, then leaped into the boma.

Things happened fast. The torch was knocked from

Roger's hand. It lay blinking in the grass. Roger tried to get his spear. It was buried under five hundred pounds of lion.

Hal, leaping about to keep clear of the lion's claws, did not dare to shoot again for fear of hitting his brother. He finally got the muzzle close to the lion's head. Then a great paw, more powerful than any baseball bat, the paw that could knock a zebra dead with one slap, struck the barrel and bent it into a V.

If Hal had fired at that instant, the gun would have exploded, killing all three, and that would have been the end of the story.

He took his finger off the trigger. As the lion lunged for him, jaws agape, he jammed the bent barrel down the beast's throat.

The lion fell over and clawed at the gun with his hind paws. He rolled about on the ground. He rid himself of the gun barrel but he got something else.

Ants.

He stood up and shook himself. He bit at his flanks and pawed his ears and throat. He dashed about the boma. He had forgotten the boys.

The ants that had tortured them promptly left them to attack their new victim. They were large for ants, almost an inch long, and had jaws like pincers.

Attacking by the thousands, they could strip an animal to the bone. They entered the throat, the eyes, the ears. One of the smallest of creatures was conquering the king of beasts.

The lion leaped out of the boma and dived into the dark. They heard him plunge into a near-by water-hole.

Roger picked up the torch and they looked themselves over. Their faces, arms, clothes, were smeared with blood. But they couldn't find where the blood came from. They had many scratches, but none deep enough to produce all this gore.

Hal breathed a sigh of relief. 'It's the lion's blood, not ours. I thought I missed, but I must have creased his skull.'

'Well, let's get out of here,' said Roger. 'I've had enough for tonight.'

'You know better than that.'

Roger did know better. He knew that when a hunter wounds a wild animal he must follow it and finish it off. He knew that a badly hurt animal cannot be allowed to go loose. It must be tracked down and put out of its pain. There is another reason. A savage beast after being wounded is far more savage than before. It would revenge itself upon the first human being it could find.

'We'll go after it in the morning,' Roger said.

'We'll go after it now. It could be fifty miles away by morning.'

'But your gun is busted.'

'We still have the spear. Come along. But first, those scratches.' He took a tube of penicillin out of his bush jacket pocket.

'Why fool with them now? They are not bad.'

'Just a little scratch from a lion's claw could kill you. Blood poisoning. Lions don't manicure their nails. They are really pretty clean animals – lick themselves all over just like a cat. But they can't get under the nails. Scraps of meat get under them and rot and become poisonous. One fellow I knew who got a light scratch from a lion's claw spent the next six months in the hospital. He was lucky. He lived.'

Hal rubbed a little of the ointment into Roger's scratches, then into his own.

'That ought to do it. Let's go.'

'How about the other lions?' Roger said. He picked up the torch and played it on the goat, or the place where the goat had been. It was gone, and so were the lions.

'Good,' he said. 'We don't have to worry about them.'

'We can't be sure of that. They may be lying near by, digesting their meal. Perhaps they're all around us. If we bump into one of them, we're in trouble. They may be harmless old pussycats if they're let alone, but they don't like to be stepped on.'

He took the spear and pushed the thorns aside at the point where the man-eater had leaped over the wall. He stepped through and Roger followed, carrying the torch.

There were deep gouges in the ground where the lion had landed. Then he had made straight for the water-hole, leaving a trail of blood. The boys followed warily, watching every rock to be sure it was a rock and not a lion. Sleepy growls came from the bushes. At the edge of the water-hole three lions that had been drinking looked into the light.

'Steady,' whispered Hal. 'No sudden moves.'

It was important to show no sign of fear. Even a well-behaved lion can't resist the temptation to chase a man who runs.

'Walk backwards,' Hal whispered.

Still facing the animals, they stepped slowly backwards along the edge of the pool. They took their time about it. If they tripped on a root or a hummock and fell the chances were good that they would not be allowed to get up again.

Hal felt he was getting cross-eyed, trying to watch the lions and at the same time watch the ground to see where the man-eater had come out of the pool. There was no use looking for footprints. The prints of lions' feet were everywhere.

They had gone halfway around the water-hole before he saw what he was looking for – pebbles stained with red, and a blood trail leading off into the jungle.

This was going to be worse than he had expected. The lion had not stayed in the open, but had crawled off into the underbrush. It might be hiding behind any bush. with an aching head and a heart full of hate. If it heard and smelled hunters approaching, it would brace itself for a spring. Lions had been known to leap twelve feet high and span a distance of forty-five feet in one jump. This one wouldn't need to do as well. Bushes pressed close on both sides – if the lion were lurking behind one he might reach his enemies with a spring of only ten feet or less.

Roger stepped on a log. It rolled, dropping him on his back, then came up on four legs and made off.

'Watch your step!' Hal said angrily as Roger picked himself up. 'Lucky that wasn't the one we're looking for.'

'Perhaps it was,' admitted Roger.

'Not a chance. He wouldn't have let you off so easily. Besides, the blood trail shows he didn't stop here.'

They followed the red-stained bushes a little farther. Then Hal stopped.

'Shine that torch down here – close.'

He examined every leaf, every twig. No sign of blood. Perhaps the wound had stopped bleeding. But that was not likely. It was more probable that the lion was right here, somewhere, behind these bushes.

He approached a bush cautiously, trying to peer through it or around it.

'Look out,' cried Roger. 'Behind you.'

Hal wheeled around. He braced himself for the lion's spring. But lions seldom do what is expected of them. There was no spring.

A pair of great yellow coals burned in the bush. Above them was a shaggy head matted with blood.

The beast was flat on the ground. He crept forward inch by inch. He did not roar, he did not cough. He purred.

It was not a friendly, catty purr. It was a dreadful thing to hear, full of anger and revenge, and it seemed to come not just from the throat but from the whole furious beast. It was like the rumbling before an earthquake.

'Give me that spear,' Roger said.

'No, I'll use it. You get back out of the way.'

'Give it to me,' insisted Roger. 'They showed me how to use it.'

'You're not strong enough.'

'It doesn't take strength.' He yanked it out of Hal's hand. 'You hold the light.'

There was no time to argue. Hal held the light. He realized with a jolt that this youngster was growing up. In ten seconds he would either be dead or he would be a man. It was Masai custom – no Masai youth was considered a man until he had killed a lion.

Roger was already regretting his burst of courage.

Those glaring yellow eyes, the tail erect and as stiff as a gun barrel, the deep deadly purr, brought the sweat out in beads on Roger's forehead. He clenched his teeth. He tried to quiet his fluttering nerves.

He was big and strong for his age—yet he knew better than to trust his own strength. He called on Mother Earth to help him. Instead of hurling the spear, he planted the butt firmly in the ground. He pointed the blade directly towards the lion's chest. He held it in that position as steadily as his dancing nerves would permit.

The final charge of a lion comes like a bolt of lightning. By comparison, a charge of an elephant or rhino or hippo or even a buffalo is slow motion.

At one instant Roger was watching a creeping animal still a good ten feet away. At the next instant it was

coming out of the bush like a bullet, but a bullet with five hundred pounds behind it.

But behind the spear was the whole weight of Mother Earth. The point penetrated the chest. The great jaws jerked down, gripped the shaft, pulled it out, and snapped it as if it had been bamboo. With a roar of rage and pain, the man-eater fell on his side, struggled to get up, fell again, and lay still.

Roger felt suddenly very young. He sat down weakly and mopped his face. Hal put his hand on the boy's trembling shoulder. He tried to speak – but the words wouldn't come.

Words were not necessary. They both knew what that touch on the shoulder meant – not the comfort given by a man to a child, but the respect of a man for a man.

4

The man-eaters of Tsavo

HAL and Roger were not happy about it. They had not wanted to kill the animal – it was just a job that had to be done.

Someone else was not happy. King Ku.

'I don't believe it,' he growled when Tanga, the station master, told him the news. 'Two boys – alone? Their crew must have helped them. I thought I gave orders...'

'Your orders were obeyed,' Tanga said. 'The boys did it alone.'

'Were they hurt?'

'The lion mauled them.'

King Ku's eyes brightened. 'Ah, that is too bad. Are they in the hospital? Will they live?'

'They will live – they did not need to go to the hospital.'

'But you say they were hurt. Soon they will find poison in their blood and they will die. It is very sad.'

'They treated the wounds with the white man's strong stuff. They will not die.'

King Ku's dark face seemed to become darker. 'We'll see about that.' Then, noticing the puzzled look on Tanga's face, he added, 'I mean, we'll see that they are protected. I'll order my medicine man to cast a spell over them. Tell them to have no fear of claws or teeth. No harm can come to them. You will tell them?'

'I will tell them.'

He did. In the dingy little railway station the boys listened to Tanga's assurance that King Ku would take care of them.

Then, leaving Tanga at his desk, they went out to walk up and down the railway platform and wonder what it all meant.

'Why is Ku so anxious to have us think we can't be hurt?' puzzled Hal. 'Is he trying to throw us off guard? Does he want us to take chances so we *will* be hurt? What can that old geezer have against us?'

'He looks savage enough to be capable of most anything,' Roger said. 'And Tanga – you know he was the one who got us into this. Do you suppose the two of them are trying to do us in?'

'Tanga seems such a good guy,' Hal said. 'Always smiling.'

'I know. But smiles don't mean much. You know what Hamlet said – about how a fellow can "smile, and smile, and be a villain".'

'Well,' Hal said, 'I'm not going to worry myself sick about it. Let's go get a little shut-eye to make up for last night.'

In their tent which had been pitched close to the railway track they tossed restlessly on their cots.

'What I can't understand,' Roger said, 'is how all this man-eating got started. Why is it so bad here?'

'You've heard of "the man-eaters of Tsavo"?'

'It sort of rings a bell. What's the story?'

'It happened right here. A couple of thousand men were building this stretch of railway. Their boss was a construction engineer named Colonel Patterson.

'Some of the men got sick and died. Colonel Patterson ordered several men to bury the dead, and paid them extra for digging the graves. The men took the money, but they were too lazy to dig graves. They just hid the corpses in the bushes.

'Game was scarce that year and the lions were hungry. Two of them found the bodies and ate them. That gave them a taste for human flesh. More men died and were eaten. The lions came every night. One night they found no corpses -- so they broke into a tent, dragged out two men, killed them, and ate them.'

Roger sat bolt upright. 'You mean they came straight into a tent – a tent like this?'

'Exactly like this. And they kept coming every night.'

'But didn't this Colonel Patterson do anything about it?'

'He tried. But remember, he was an engineer, not a hunter. He had plenty of courage, but he didn't quite know how to go about it. He would sit up in a tree with a gun near the spot where a man had been killed the night before. The lions had too much sense to go there again. They would attack somewhere else.

'One night he sat up on a branch above the body of a man who had just died. Having been up every night, the colonel was very tired. He went to sleep. A growl below disturbed him, he moved a little, and fell plop on to a lion. Luckily the lion was so startled that it ran off into the bush.

'The colonel built a lion trap. It was a big box made out of wood and iron and the door was fixed so it would close and lock if a spring in the floor was stepped on. At the back of the box he fenced off a small room and put a couple of men in it. They were safe behind bars. The idea was that the lion would come into the cage after the men and would step on the spring and lock himself in.

'One of the man-eaters did walk into the trap, stepped on the spring, and the door snapped shut. The lion roared and woke the camp. The colonel and four of his men with rifles came running and fired twenty bullets into the cage. They couldn't see very well – they missed the lion but one of their bullets broke the latch, the door swung open, and the lion escaped.

'The colonel tried tin pans. He had his men surround a man-eater where it lay in the brush. Each man was armed with several tin pans. A passage was left open for the lion to escape. There the colonel posted himself so that he could pot the lion when it came out of the brush.

'When he was all ready the men beat their tin pans together and the frightened lion came running through the brush. The colonel pulled the trigger but the gun only clicked. A misfire. Before he could use the other barrel the lion got away.

'The colonel didn't get much help from his men because they believed the lions were really devils and could not be killed.

'The lions did show devilish intelligence. The colonel had strychnine put in the corpses of two men and laid them out in the bush. The lions were heard prowling about during the night but in the morning the bodies were still there, untouched. But two more men were missing from the camp.

'More than a thousand of the men went on strike.

They leaped on a train bound for Mombasa.

'The men who were left built shelters for themselves up on tanks or roofs or in trees. Some dug pits under their tents, covered the pits with logs, and slept down in the hole. Surely there they would be safe. But the lions pulled aside the logs, leaped down into the pits, and dragged out the men.

'They didn't take the trouble to pull them off into the brush but ate them just outside the tents in spite of a hail of bullets.

'So many men climbed one tree that it fell on a man-eater, pinning him to the ground, but before they could call the colonel with his gun the lion wriggled loose and disappeared.

'Two experienced hunters came down from Nairobi. They had shot plenty of lions and were sure they could get these two devils. As soon as they stepped from the train a lion leaped upon one of them, knocked him down, and proceeded to eat him. When the other hunter attempted to interfere the lion jumped on his back and ripped it to shreds. The hunter was taken to the hospital. He never did shoot that lion.

'One night a dead donkey was put out where the lions could easily get at it. The colonel had a hunting platform —they call it a *machan* – put up about ten feet from the body. The machan was twelve feet high and consisted of four poles stuck into the ground and supporting a plank that served as a seat.

'The colonel perched up on this seat, gun in hand. A little after midnight he heard a sigh – a lion often sighs when he is hungry. The rustling in the dark told the colonel that the beast was close to the donkey. The colonel tried to keep quiet – but as he raised his gun it bumped against the plank and the lion at once left the donkey and began circling around the man.

'For two hours the horrified colonel heard the beast creeping round and round in the darkness, gradually coming closer. At any moment he expected the lion to rush the machan and perhaps break one of the flimsy poles and bring the whole thing to the ground.

'Suddenly something came flop against the back of the colonel's head. He was so terrified that he nearly fell off the plank. He thought the lion had leaped upon him from behind. Then he realized it had only been an owl which had perhaps mistaken him for the branch of a tree.

'His sudden movement when the owl struck him made the plank creak. The lion heard the sound and came growling up to the machan. There was just enough dawn light so that Colonel Patterson could see the dark form against the whitish undergrowth.

'He took careful aim and fired. The lion let out a terrific roar and began leaping about in all directions. The roars died down to groans and the groans to deep sighs – then nothing.

'Men from the camp a quarter of a mile away came running and when they saw that the "devil" was dead they beat tom-toms and blew horns and threw themselves down on the ground before Colonel Patterson crying, *"Mabarak! Mabarak!"* It means "Blessed One" or "Saviour". They were sure the colonel must be some sort of god to have conquered this devil.

'But there was still the other man-eater to be reckoned with. It tried to get into the station where some men were sleeping, but the doors were too strong. It climbed up on the roof and tore away the corrugated iron sheets —it made a hole and dropped through. The men decided in a hurry that it was safer outside than in. They ran out, the lion after them.

'One man hid in a water-tank. The lion upset the tank, pulled the unlucky fellow out, and ate him.

'Then a very important man, Superintendent Ryall of the Railway Police, arrived in his own private railway car. He was a good shot and he knew it. He thought he could do in a day what Colonel Patterson had failed to do in nine months. Just give him one chance at that man-eater.

'He got his chance. He had his car shunted to a siding, and with two friends, Hübner and Parenti, prepared to wait all night for the lion. If they heard him grunting around, they would just go out and kill him. It would be as simple as that.

'One would keep watch while the other two slept. Ryall took the first watch, but he fell asleep. Hübner suddenly woke and found to his horror that the lion was inside the car. It had pushed open the sliding door and jumped in. The door slid back and closed.

'The lion leaped up on Ryall's bed, struck the sleeping man's head with his paw, sank its teeth into his chest, and that was the end of Ryall. The lion dragged the body off on to the floor and in doing so he disturbed Parenti, who woke to find a quarter of a ton of lion on top of him.

'Hübner jumped over the lion and got to the door. He couldn't open it. The reason was that men who had been roused by the commotion were holding it shut so that the lion would not escape into the camp.

'It must have been a bad shock for those two fellows to find themselves shut in with a man-eating lion. Hübner groped for his gun, but before he could find it there was a terrific crash – the lion had broken through a window taking Ryall's body with him.

'The next day a search was made for the police officer's body. Nothing was found but his boots.

'It was Colonel Patterson after all, the man who was not a good shot, who finally potted the second man-eater. The animal tried to get at some men sleeping in a tree. The next night Patterson was up in that tree. The lion came, tried to climb the tree, and was shot. He roared off into the bushes. In the morning Patterson went looking for him.

'He saw what looked like a dead lion – but the "dead lion" suddenly came to life and charged him.

'The beast was too weak from loss of blood to finish the charge. He died only five yards from Patterson's feet.

'Those two lions alone had killed more than a hundred men including twenty-nine Indians and two Europeans. The story was told and retold hundreds of times in newspapers and magazines all over the world. The two skins were mounted and put on view in the Field Museum and if you ever go to Chicago you can see them there.'

'But you haven't answered my question,' Roger said. 'Those lions are dead. But still we have man-eaters here. Why is that?'

'For a very simple reason. The man-eaters of Tsavo often brought their cubs along and taught them how to hunt man and enjoy human flesh. Those cubs when they grew up taught their cubs. And so it goes on.'

'Why doesn't it happen in other places too?'

'It does. Lions are the greatest man-killers in Africa. Not long ago in Malawi fourteen persons were eaten by lions in a month; in Mozambique, twenty in one month; in Ankole over in Uganda a dozen lions went on the rampage and it took eighteen months to kill them off. Near Entebbe the wise old lions discovered that whenever elephants raided plantations the people would come out to drive them away and in the confusion the lions could easily grab a few victims. Seventeen lions had to be killed before the people were safe. In Sanga a single lion killed forty-four people and another took eighty-five. It will go on as long as there are any lions.'

'Then why not get rid of all lions?'

'That's like saying why not get rid of all motor cars. They cause a lot more deaths than the lions do. The lion is one of the most magnificent animals we have on this planet. People come from all over the world to see him. And even if lions kill one or two hundred Africans in a year that's not many out of a population of three hundred million. Of course we don't want them to get even one hundred. It's not much comfort to a woman whose husband has been killed to know that most lions are not dangerous. Get your beauty sleep. We've got to find another of these rascals tomorrow morning.'

5

The lion that snored

THEY didn't have to wait until morning.

Roger no sooner got to sleep than he was wakened by a snoring sound. That was strange. His brother never snored.

Could it be one of the railway men in the next tent? But it was closer than that. It must be Hal.

Roger hated to wake him up. His brother had had a hard day and needed his sleep. Roger tried to ignore the noise. He just buried his ears, one in the pillow and the other under the covers.

It was no use. He couldn't get to sleep with that racket going on. He was just about to speak when he heard Hal's voice.

'Roger. Wake up. You're snoring loud enough to wake the whole camp.'

'I wasn't snoring,' Roger protested.

'Guess you weren't – because I still hear it. Must be a hyena prowling around outside.'

'If it's a hyena it's not outside. It's right here between us.'

'We'll soon see,' Hal said and turned on his torch.

There *was* something between the two cots but it was a lot bigger than a hyena. There stood a super-size lion. He had a black mane. He looked remarkably like the beast they *thought* they had killed.

The loose tent flaps showed how he had entered. He was growling softly. He looked from one boy to the other, trying to decide which would make a better supper.

Hal grabbed for his gun. He had left a ·45 revolver lying on a camp chair between the two beds so that either he or Roger could reach it in case of trouble.

The lion got there first. Excited by Hal's sudden movement, he struck out with his paw, knocking over the chair and spinning the revolver to the back of the tent.

Then he chose Roger, perhaps because he looked more tender than his tough older brother, or because he was in the full light of the torch while Hal was in the shadow.

There was plenty of action crowded into the next few seconds. The lion clawed at the covers. Roger locked them under his body so they could not be torn off. The lion's jaws opened within inches of his face. The big black nose almost touched his own.

If the lion could bite, so could he. He sank his teeth into the lion's nose. At the same instant, Hal was pulling the animal's tail. This was a favourite Masai trick. The two tenderest parts of a lion are the nose and the tail.

Roger looked for some weapon. There was nothing – nothing but a few groceries on a shelf above his cot. Desperate, he grabbed a half-used box of pancake flour and dashed the contents into the lion's eyes.

The animal looked like a comedian that has just been plastered with a custard pie. Roger would have laughed, if this had been a moment for laughing.

This lion had probably fought many battles but he had never before been attacked with pancake flour. Surprised and blinded, he roared his disapproval. He tore loose from the nose-hold and tail-hold and plunged out of the tent. He took with him what could have been Roger's body but was actually only a fat pillow. It had the smell of a human, but when he tore it apart and found no flesh and bones he again roared in bitter disappointment.

Hal jumped for his gun. 'That beast is going to kill somebody as soon as he gets the flour out of his eyes. He's rarin' mad.'

Hal found his revolver and tossed another to Roger. Revolvers were better than rifles for a close-range job like this one.

In pyjamas and bare feet, they burst out of the tent. The torch revealed the scattered fragments of the pillow. But there was no lion.

A scream came from the next tent. Hal turned his torch upon it in time to see the lion rush out dragging the struggling body of a man. His entire head was locked between the animal's jaws.

Wrestling with his victim, the lion paid no attention to Hal and Roger. They fired. The light was poor. But they did see the lion fall.

Men who had been roused by the beast's roars and the screams of his victim poured from the other tents.

Some carried torches, others waved pangas, the long heavy knives that are used to cut brush or kill enemies.

They found Hal on the ground bending over the man's bloody body with his ear against the chest. He rose slowly and spoke. Since the British had so long ruled Kenya these black workers knew enough English to understand Hal when he said simply, 'He's gone.'

They looked at the lion, its face still white.

'You see,' said one. 'Ghost ... devil ... it pretends to be dead ... these lions that kill us ... you cannot kill them.'

Hal walked over to the lion and wiped some of the white from its face.

'No ghost,' he said. 'Just a lion – and very dead.'

There was a job to be done – a body to be buried. He played his torch over the ground, looking for the lion's victim. It had disappeared.

'Where is it?' he demanded.

A man answered, 'It all right – you no worry.'

'Did you bury it?'

'We take care. You never mind.'

'I want to know – are you going to dig a grave?'

'Grave too much hard work. We railway men. We

work much all day. No spend night digging graves.'

'Then what did you do?'

'Him over there,' pointing to some bushes.

'Don't you know that's the worst thing you can do?' Hal said.

He strode over to the bushes. An angry snarl greeted him. The body was half hidden under the head and shoulders of a large lioness. Beside the lioness was a little cub, its paws up on the dead man's chest.

It was the same old story over again. The mother was giving her cub his first lesson in man-eating.

The lioness looked up, growled, and braced herself for a spring. She had two reasons to be annoyed. She had been disturbed before she could begin her dinner. And she feared for the safety of her cub.

The railway men, armed only with pangas, scattered like leaves before a storm and left Hal and Roger alone to face the queen of beasts.

What should they do? To kill a female with cubs was against all the rules of sportsmanship. And yet, if this old lady were not done away with no railway worker would be safe.

Hal did not have to decide. The lioness decided for him. Flexing her muscles to turn them into steel springs, she left the ground and the great bulk of her came flying through the air straight for Hal's throat.

He dodged, tripped over a root, and fell flat in the bushes.

The lioness was on him in a flash, tearing at his pyjamas.

Roger danced around, trying to get in a shot, but fearing he would hit his brother instead of the beast. He tore

off his pyjama coat and clamped it against the animal's eyes. The lioness backed up to free herself of the blindfold, then turned her attention to Roger. Her sledgehammer paw struck him on the hip, spilling him into the grass, but in the split second before he fell his bullet caught her between the eyes.

Hearing the shot, some men came running and saw a spectacle that amused them no end. The two bold hunters were both on the ground, one on top of the other, and on top of both was a dead lioness.

They helped disentangle the heap of hunters and hunted and got the boys on their feet. Now there were more scratches to be attended to, deeper ones than before. The boys wobbled towards their tent. Hal turned his flashlight on the spot where Black Mane had fallen. There was no lion – only some blood and pancake flour on the grass. Hunters had told Hal that it sometimes takes a dozen shots to kill a lion. He began to believe it.

The hunters collapsed on their cots. Hal reached to the shelf above him and got the sulphonamide powder. He rose wearily and rubbed the powder deep into his brother's cuts. Roger did the same for him, and in doing so he stumbled over an object on the ground. He turned the light on it. It was the cub.

The little beast, too young to know a friend from an enemy, had left its dead protector to follow the living. It miaowed in quite cat-like fashion when Roger's foot touched it. Roger took it up in his arms.

'Poor little brat,' he said. 'Sorry we had to bop off your mama.'

'Don't start getting sentimental over that thing,' Hal warned. 'We may have to knock him off.'

'You wouldn't do that.'

'Oh yes I would – if he's had enough lessons so he's on his way to becoming a man-eater.'

'Can't we test him? You have a nice bloody hand – put it under his nose and see what he does about it.'

The cub stretched his head forward, sniffed at the hand and seemed about to lick the blood. Then he turned his head away and miaowed again.

'You see?' Roger said triumphantly. 'He's no man-eater. He'd rather have milk.'

'He's not starving,' Hal said. 'His mother probably gave him a drink a little while ago. Tie him up and leave him here for a spell. We have a job to do.'

6

Basa, son of Basa

THEY came out into the first light of dawn.

Most of the men had retired to their tents. A few still stood around, pangas in hand, discussing the exciting events of the night and warily watching for another man-eater.

'Do any of you know,' Hal said, 'where the man came from – the man who was killed?'

'Yes,' said one. 'From Gula.'

'Is it far?'

'No. Only ten minutes.'

'Then why hasn't anyone gone to tell his family?'

The men stared at Hal as if he had said something ridiculous. Then they laughed. The roar of a lion came from the woods. 'That's why,' someone said.

Hal had to admit it was a good reason. Who could be expected to go walking down a forest trail at the risk of meeting a man-eater around any turn?

He spoke to the man who knew the way to Gula. 'We have guns – we will go with you.'

The man reluctantly agreed. They set out for the village of Gula. It was still dark in the woods and Hal played his torch on the path.

Occasionally they heard the voice of a lion – but it

was an after-dinner roar – not the before-dinner grunt of a hungry lion.

'Sounds as if they've already eaten,' Hal said. 'We're safe enough.'

Roger hoped so, but he kept a nervous look-out. It was a relief when the path left the woods and climbed a low hill to a dozen mud-and-thatch huts.

A woman was out gathering firewood. Hal's guide asked her, 'Where is the home of Basa?'

'Over yonder. Why! Is there bad news?'

'Basa has been killed by a lion.'

The woman dropped her wood, ran screaming to the hut of Basa and beat on the door.

The door opened to reveal a tall, powerful-looking young African of about Hal's own age. In a corner a woman bent over a fire burning on the earthen floor. Two small children stopped their play and stared at the strangers.

You could tell when a young man had been to school. This one had. Hal addressed him in English.

'You are the son of Basa?'

'I am.'

'We have very sad news for you. Your father has been attacked by a lion.'

'You mean – he is dead?'

'He is dead. You will come?'

The son of Basa turned and spoke to his mother in the tribal language. She slowly rose to her feet and stood looking at him as if paralysed. She said nothing.

The men left the hut. They were halfway down the hill before they heard the wailing cry of the widow of Basa. It was not a pleasant sound and they hurried on.

As they went, Hal introduced himself and his brother. He got no friendly response from young Basa.

'I know who you are,' said the young African. 'You were brought here to stop the killing of men. You have not stopped it. You allowed my father to be killed.'

Hal tried to explain. 'We did what we could. The lion came first into our tent.'

'So you had a chance to shoot it. Why didn't you shoot it?'

'It knocked our revolver out of reach.'

Young Basa snorted. 'That is a poor excuse. Your gun should be always with you.'

'You are right,' admitted Hal. He was beginning to feel very guilty about the whole thing.

'Then what?' demanded Basa.

'The lion attacked my brother. He blinded it with flour.'

'And you—' said Basa. 'Why weren't you getting your gun while this was going on?'

Hal didn't like being quizzed by this angry young man, but he kept his temper.

'It all happened so fast. The lion grabbed a pillow and ran out.'

'So you had a good chance to get your guns.'

'We got them and jumped out. The lion was already dragging your father out of the next tent.'

'I have heard you,' snapped Basa. 'It is as if you had murdered him. I should kill you now. But that must wait until my father is in his grave.'

Poor fellow, thought Hal, he's upset. That's what makes him so unreasonable.

But while he tried to put the blame on young Basa, he

was painfully aware that he and his brother had bungled this thing very badly. Great hunters, they were! Couldn't even pot a cat when it walked in and asked to be killed. He felt a burning sense of shame.

And a certain fear, for he knew Basa's words were not just words. It was a tradition of this land that a son must not rest until he had avenged the death of his father.

Hal seemed to be collecting enemies instead of friends. Now he had to watch four ways. He needed eyes on four sides of his head – a pair to look for man-eaters, another pair for King Ku who appeared to have some sort of grudge against him, a pair for Tanga who was under Ku's orders, and a pair that really should be focused night and day on angry young Basa.

No, not four pairs, but five. There must be one more enemy. Who had loosened the flaps of the tent so the lion could enter? He was sure they had been firmly tied before they went to bed.

The flaps of the next tent were also loose – but that was because the lion's roars had brought a man from that tent to join the rest who came out to see what all the roaring was about. Then the lion had plunged in to seize Basa's father.

But that didn't explain why Hal's tent flaps were open. A lion could not untie knots – then who had done this, and why?

7

The sorehead

YOUNG Basa strode into the camp of the railway men and stood looking down upon his father.

His black face seemed to become even blacker with grief and anger.

Then he picked up the body, slung it over his powerful young shoulders, and, without a word to anyone, went off up the trail to his village.

The men were having their breakfast around open-air fires. Soon they would be going to work on the tracks. Hal's eye wandered over them and he wondered sadly which one of them would be taken today.

Then, far down the camp-ground beyond all the black workers he thought he saw a white face. Who could that be? Hal decided he would go down and say hello. He liked the Africans well enough but it would be pleasant to talk with someone of his own kind.

He looked around for Roger but that young man had gone to the tent to take care of his cub.

Hal strolled down through the camp-ground. The stranger saw him coming and walked off rapidly along the tracks.

Hal stopped short. It was plain that the fellow didn't want to see him.

Now Hal's curiosity was really aroused. Perhaps the station master could tell him about the new arrival.

In the station he found Tanga already at his desk, a cup of tea at his elbow.

'I see we have a white visitor,' Hal said. 'Caught a glimpse of him in the camp.'

'Yes,' said Tanga. 'He came in yesterday on the afternoon train.'

'Who is he?'

'A white hunter. His name is Dugan.'

'What does he want here?'

Tanga shifted in his chair. 'I don't think that concerns you.'

'But I think it does. If a man won't stand and talk to me, that concerns me. What does he have against me?'

'Well, as a matter of fact, Mr Hunt ... you took his job.'

'How in the world did I do that? I don't even know the fellow. I never saw him before in my life.'

Tanga settled back and looked up at the ceiling. 'I don't suppose there's any harm in telling you. About a month ago we began to have trouble with man-eaters. Dugan had helped us before, so we called him in. He went gunning for the lions and he killed some but evidently not the right ones. We kept right on losing men. So that's why I went to the warden and he recommended you. We fired Dugan. He's very sore about it, I'm afraid. He came yesterday and wanted his job back.'

'He's welcome to it,' Hal said promptly. 'We're not

doing so well with it ourselves. You know there was another man killed last night.'

'Yes, I know. But you've only been on the job two days. Anyhow, I refused to take him back. I thought he would get out of here on the night train. But he's still hanging around. I think he means mischief. Look out for him. He's hoping you will fail – and he'll help you fail, if he can. He wouldn't stop at anything.'

Hal thought of the loose tent flaps. He was sure that neither he nor Roger could have left them open. Even a very smart lion couldn't untie them. Perhaps this sorehead had done it.

Hal said nothing about it to Tanga. After all, it was a serious matter – to accuse a man of attempted murder. He would just keep quiet and see what happened next.

He went back to his tent.

Roger was trying to give his cub a drink.

He had placed a pan of water on the floor. Now he was pressing the cub's nose down into the water.

Hal laughed. 'What are you trying to do – drown your cub?'

'He must be thirsty. Why doesn't he drink?'

'Why does he have to be thirsty?' Hal asked.

'Because all animals are. Listen, don't tell me about pets. I've had leopards and baboons and a baby elephant and a cheetah. They were all heavy drinkers.'

'But you haven't had a lion,' Hal said. 'Don't you know a lion can go a week without water? You might almost think he's a cousin to the camel.'

'But every animal has to have moisture.'

'Right. But he doesn't have to get it from a water-hole or river.'

'Then where does he get it?'

'From the animals he eats. An antelope's body is more than half water. The lion eats the antelope and gets all the liquid he needs.'

'But this little chump isn't old enough to catch antelopes.'

'True. But Nature takes care of that. Until he's old enough to hunt, his mother's milk gives him both food and liquid.'

'Funny he doesn't like water.'

'He loves water. Let go of him and see what he does.'

Roger released the cub which immediately slapped its big flat front paws into the pan, splashing water in all directions. The hind paws followed. The paws were too large for the animal. They reminded Roger of snow-shoes, or big floppy fins on the feet of a skin-diver. The little beast would have to grow before he would catch up with the size of his paws. They went slap-slap-slap in the shallow water.

'What are you going to call him?' Hal asked.

Roger watched his cub flopping about on those furry, over-sized pads, and said, 'There's only one name for him. Flop.'

Flop flopped over on his back and waved all four snow-shoes in the air. He rolled about in the water with evident enjoyment.

'Now there's another funny thing,' Roger said. 'He won't drink it but he likes to be in it. He's crazy. Doesn't he knows that cats don't like to get wet?'

'He doesn't follow all the cat rules. A lion likes to play in the water and he's a good swimmer.'

Flop bounced out of the pan, climbed up on Roger's knee, and whacked the boy's face with one big, soaking-wet paw. The blow was almost hard enough to make Roger see stars.

'Hey, cut that out.' Roger wiped his face with the sleeve of his bush-jacket.

'He's just playing,' Hal said. 'You'll have to get used to that if you want to make a pal of a lion. They love to play – but they don't know their own strength.'

Now the affectionate little beast was licking Roger's hand. His tongue was like sandpaper. Three licks, and Roger was beginning to lose his skin. He withdrew his hand.

'Before this monster eats me up,' he said, 'we'd better

give it some food. How do we get some mother's milk?'

'This will have to do,' Hal said. He took down a can of milk, opened it, and held it under Flop's nose. The cub raised his nose in the air and said, 'Ng-ng-ng.'

'If I'm not mistaken,' Hal said, 'that's lion language for "No". Perhaps if we warm the milk he'll think better of it.'

After the milk was warmed on the little camp stove, another problem arose. How to get the milk into the cub.

Some was poured into a dish and placed before the animal. Flop sniffed it and apparently wanted it, but didn't know how to get it. Roger pressed the cub's mouth down into the milk. The cub jerked his head free, scattering drops of milk from his whiskers. He had not learned how to lap up liquid in cat fashion. He was used to sucking his dinner from his mother's teats.

Roger got a spoon. 'If you'll hold him,' he said, 'I can spoon the milk into his mouth.'

'That's force-feeding,' Hal said. 'He should be fed every three hours. To feed him that way would take too much of our time – besides, no animal likes to be forced. We've got to give him an artificial mother. He's used to sucking his dinner. Now how can we let him suck?'

'If we had a piece of rubber tubing—'

'But we haven't.'

'I know what,' Roger said. 'There's an artificial mother right back of the tent.'

He went out and came back in a moment with a stem of bamboo about a half inch in diameter. He cut it down to a length of a few inches and looked through it to make sure that it was not closed by any partition. He rounded off the upper end so that it would be comfortable in the cub's mouth. Then he put one end in the little animal's mouth and the other end in the milk.

The little beast instinctively sucked and up came the milk. He clamped the hollow bamboo between his two front paws and settled down contently to his dinner.

Roger saw that Flop was not gripping the tube with his toe-nails but with a claw a little farther up on the inside of each leg.

'I didn't know a lion had claws up there,' Roger said.

'They're called dew-claws,' said Hal.

'What are they for? They're too far up to touch the ground.'

'And yet, they're the best claws a lion has, and the most dangerous. On a full-grown lion they can be two inches long. They're usually kept folded against the lion's legs, but the lion can extend them at right angles. They are as sharp as razors and very strong. A lion can rip a man open with one stroke of these terrible hooks.'

'But the cub is using them to hold the tube.'

'Yes. And when he grows up he'll use them to hold his meat while he eats it. They're something like a man's thumbs. Just as you couldn't hold anything without your thumbs, a lion would have trouble hanging on to anything without his dew-claws. So you see, the lion is well armed. But when he closes his mouth to hide those terrific fangs of his, and draws up his claws, and folds in his dews-claws, he looks as if he wouldn't hurt a fly.'

'Does he have any other concealed weapons.'

'One more. Feel the end of your cub's tail.'

Roger did so. 'Ouch!' he exclaimed. 'He's got a needle there.' It was hidden in the little tuft of black hair at the end of the youngster's tail. 'What's the idea of that?'

'Just to protect his rear. The lion is a great tail-switcher. If an enemy comes up too close behind him it is apt to get punctured by that needle. It hurts like the sting of a hornet.'

The kitten, finishing his milk, looked up and miaowed. It was hard to believe that this innocent little thing would become the king of beasts, the terror of the jungle.

Hal reached down and rubbed the cat behind the ears. It responded as any house cat would, with a purr. The purr was like a deep note played on an organ.

'I'll show you another catty thing a lion does,' Hal said. 'Give me that bottle of after-shave lotion.'

'You're not going to shave Flop.'

'Never fear.' He took out his handkerchief and sprinkled some drops of lotion on it. He put the perfumed handkerchief on the ground under Flop's nose.

Flop flipped. The fragrance sent him into a complete tailspin. He rolled on the handkerchief, sniffing, moaning, and gurgling. He seemed to be chuckling with delight. He rubbed his cheeks into the sweet-smelling handkerchief.

'Just like a cat with catnip,' Roger said.

'Exactly like a cat,' Hal agreed. 'He'd behave much the same way over catnip but he likes perfume better.'

'What is there about perfume to send him into such a tizzy?'

'Doesn't it do the same to human beings – more or less? At least, they enjoy it. Funny thing – it doesn't excite the girl lion so much. It's the boy lion who really falls apart. And it isn't true of all the big cats. The leopard or the tiger can take it or leave it. Perhaps the lion is more closely related than they are to the house cat.'

It would have been pleasant to play with Flop all day, but there were more important things to be done.

Leashing Flop to the leg of a bed and leaving him to enjoy his shaving lotion, they set out on their quest for man-eaters.

Where should they look? The railway workers were scattered along three miles of track. It was impossible for the boys to see what was happening three miles away, or even one mile or a half mile off.

In fact a lion might be lying in the grass only a few hundred yards distant and not be seen. A lion can flatten himself almost to the ground and remain perfectly still for long periods of time. His brown fur is like the brown grass all around him, and if he wears a patch of black it looks like a bush.

The boys climbed to the roof of the station and used their binoculars.

'It's no good,' Hal said. 'We're not high enough. A lion could be behind any one of those thorn bushes. Or behind that tall grass. Or behind an ant-hill.'

They climbed down again. There seemed nothing to do but to start at one end and patrol the track to the other end of the three-mile stretch.

They slowly walked the track, guns in hand, Hal keeping watch on one side and Roger on the other. As they went by the camp-ground they happened to see Dugan come out of his tent. He also carried a gun. He stopped when he saw the boys and struck off in another direction.

It was slow and careful work, examining every tuft of

grass to be sure it was not a lion, asking the men along the way if they had seen anything, looking for the footprints of big cats.

They had not been at it more than half an hour when a man came running down the track crying, '*Simba!*'* The boys ran to meet him. The man fell to the ground, gasping, trying to get his breath back, and pointing down the track.

'How far?' Hal asked.

'Five minutes fast.' Africans did not measure distance in miles but in time. Five minutes fast meant the distance you could cover in that time if you went on the run.

The boys ran. It was a good mile before they came upon a cluster of men looking at something on the ground. They pressed through the crowd and found what they had dreaded to find – a dead man, victim of the claws and jaws of a lion.

'Did you see the lion?' Hal asked the foreman of the gang.

'I saw,' said the foreman. 'A very great lion, brown on the sides, black as night on top.'

It must be Black Mane, thought Hal.

'Where were you?' said the foreman bitterly. 'You never here when we need you.'

'We can't be everywhere at the same time,' Hal said.

'But your man – he was near, but he did not come and shoot.'

Hal was puzzled. 'Our man? We have no man.'

'Your Dugan man. He work for you, yes?'

'No, he does not.'

A chorus of angry voices greeted this statement. The

* Lion.

men plainly did not believe Hal. They blamed him for what 'his man' had done or failed to do.

Why had Dugan not shot the lion? Why had he allowed it to take another victim?

Probably out of spite. Spite because he hadn't been hired. He wasn't being paid to kill lions so why should he bother? It was a chance to make Hal and Roger look foolish. There they had been, the idiots, in the wrong place, while a man was being killed somewhere else. If the station master had any sense he would fire these two dumb-bells and take back Dugan. And to

bring this about Dugan was willing to stand by and let a man be killed.

The boys went back to report to Tanga. The station master looked very grim as Hal explained that Dugan had been on the scene while Hal and Roger were a mile away down the track.

It wasn't pleasant to admit another failure – and to admit that if the job had been Dugan's the lion might now be dead.

'Perhaps I was wrong in letting him go,' said Tanga, as if thinking to himself. 'I'll have to report this to King Ku. He will not be pleased.'

With heavy hearts, Hal and Roger came out of the station and loitered on the platform, wondering what to do now.

'We ought to be where we could see that whole three miles of track,' Hal said.

'To do that we'd have to be sitting up on a cloud,' replied Roger bitterly.

Hal looked at his brother thoughtfully. 'You have an idea there. That's what we'll do – sit up on a cloud.'

'Are you kidding?'

'No, I'm not kidding. Come on. We'll go get the Stork.'

8

The balloon

THE Stork was the small aeroplane belonging to Mark
Crosby, warden of the Tsavo animal reserve. Hal had
flown it many times while helping Crosby clear out the
poachers who had been slaughtering the wildlife of Tsavo.

The Land-Rover made short work of the twenty miles
to Crosby's safari camp. The warden greeted the boys
warmly.

'Good to see you again. How's it going? How many
man-eaters have you knocked off?'

'Only one,' Hal said. 'In fact we're doing so badly we
expect to be fired at any moment.'

'What seems to be the trouble?'

'Too big a territory. While we're patrolling one area, a
lion kills a man somewhere else.'

'But why do you leave your crew here? If you had
your thirty men with you, they could spread out and
cover the entire territory.'

'I know,' Hal said. 'But King Ku won't allow that. He
says we must do the job alone.'

'A pretty sure way to get you killed,' Crosby said.

'But why should he want to get us killed? We haven't
done anything to annoy him.'

'You're alive, and that annoys him. You're white, and
that annoys him. Don't ask me why – I don't know. It's

some secret having to do with his past. Perhaps you'll learn what it is, if you live long enough. He's a very strange and bitter man. His wife and children were murdered in the Mau Mau rebellion. Perhaps that may have something to do with it. But why he should pick on you I don't know.'

'Well, we'll just have to make the best of it,' Hal said. 'The men are working on three miles of track. If we were up high enough we could watch the whole stretch. We wondered if you could lend us the Stork.'

Crosby tapped the desk with his pencil as he thought this over.

'Of course I can,' he said finally. 'But I'm not sure it's just what you need. An aeroplane motor makes an infernal racket. It will scare off any man-eater. By the time you land and are ready to shoot, he'll be gone. A helicopter would be better, but it's noisy too. How about a balloon?'

Hal laughed. 'Where would we get a balloon?'

'Easy enough. You've heard of Leal's balloon safari?'

Hal nodded. Stories about it had been running in the Nairobi and Mombasa papers. Leal, an Englishman, had been drifting over East Africa in a balloon, taking photographs of the animals. Used to looking at the ground, they rarely noticed the balloon, even when it hung only a hundred feet above them. It made no sound, and unless Leal and his two companions spoke there was nothing to disturb the animals grazing or resting or prowling beneath.

'A balloon would be perfect,' Hal said. 'But why should Leal lend us his balloon?'

'He won't, but I will. He has returned to England, but

just before he left he made us a present of the balloon for observation work in Tsavo – just to be sure that those poachers you scared out don't come back. It's anchored down near Mzima Springs right now. Would you care to go down and take a look at it?'

The offer was eagerly accepted. A short ride south, and there was the balloon hovering over open country along the Tsavo River and the large water-hole known as Mzima Springs. The trail line was lashed to a great stump, holding the balloon firmly in place. A nylon rope ladder reached from the basket to the ground. In the basket stood an African ranger with a pair of binoculars glued to his eyes. From this vantage, as high as the roof of a ten-storey building, he could keep watch over some ten square miles of territory.

At the foot of the ladder stood another ranger with his bicycle, ready to ride back and give the alarm if poachers were sighted.

At a signal from Crosby, the look-out climbed down.

'Not room in the basket for four,' the warden explained. 'Let's go up.'

They climbed the swaying rope ladder and stepped into the basket.

It was truly a basket with woven sides and bottom and you could see through the cracks. It wobbled and bounced as they came down into it. It was a rather close fit, little more than three feet square.

Eight ropes fastened to the edge of the basket rose to a ring and from the ring twelve lines went up to the balloon itself. The balloon, said Crosby, was about forty feet in diameter.

'What holds it up?' Roger asked. 'Hot air?'

'No,' Crosby said. 'A hot-air balloon with the same lifting ability would have to be more than three times as large. Coal gas would do better and helium even better. But the best lift comes from hydrogen and that's what is in that bag. Hydrogen is the lightest gas known. It is fourteen times as light as air.'

Roger looked up. It struck him as odd that the bottom of the bag was open. There was a hole big enough for a man to crawl through.

'Doesn't the gas ever come out through that hole?' he asked.

'No, because the gas, being light, tries to go up, never down.'

'So if we weren't tied to that stump we'd go up.'

'We certainly would.'

'And how could we make the thing come down?'

'There's a way to do that. This is a valve line. It goes right through the balloon to a valve at the top of the bag. Pull that cord and it lets a little of the gas out and the balloon will stop going up. Let out a little more gas and it will slowly come down. You can quit any time when you are low enough to suit you.'

'Of course you lose some gas that way,' said Hal. 'Suppose you want to go up again. What do you do?'

'See these bags under your feet? They're full of sand. You throw out enough sand to lighten the load and up you go. You start out with seventy of those small bags of sand. You can rise to any height you like, according to the amount of sand you toss out.'

'It sounds easy,' Roger said.

'I don't want to fool you,' the warden replied. 'It isn't easy. It's really a very tricky business. The air is full of currents going up or down or crosswise. A plane would just plough through them, bumping a little. But a balloon has no motor – it goes where the wind goes, up or down or across. If there's a strong down-draught, you may not be able to throw out sand fast enough to keep it from striking the ground. If you get caught in an up-draught you may let out too much gas so that when you get out of the draught you haven't enough to hold you up and you drop like a stone. You have to watch that altimeter all the time. Of course you won't have these troubles so long as the balloon is anchored to the ground as it is now. But if the trail line comes loose, or anybody cuts it, you're in real trouble unless you know how to navigate this crazy craft.'

Hal thought of certain persons who might like to cut the trail line. Roger thought of nothing but the delightful sensation of floating in a basket high above the earth.

It was a new experience for both boys. Planes were an old story to them. Hal had grown up with his father's private plane and was a qualified pilot. Roger was as much at home in a plane as on the ground. Ballooning was the oldest method of air travel, and yet to them it was the newest. It was an entirely fresh experience.

It seemed surprising that there was no engine roar. The silence was astonishing. There was no sound but the whisper of the breeze through the rigging or the creak of the basket under their feet.

When you were shut up in a plane's cabin it was almost like being on the ground. But here, standing in the open air, looking away without even a pane of glass between you and the landscape, able to see up to the sky past the balloon or over the edge of the basket straight down to the ground, you felt as free as a bird in space or a passenger on a Magic Carpet.

'Does this balloon have a name?' Roger asked.

'There it is, on that banner tied to the bag.'

The name was *Jules Verne*.

'Leal must have been a fan of Jules Verne,' Crosby said. 'You remember Verne's famous book, *Five weeks in a balloon*. Leal must have liked it, for he has framed one quotation from it and here it is on the inside of the basket.'

The boys crouched down and read the paragraph from *Five weeks in a balloon*:

'If I'm too hot, I go up; if I'm cold, I come down. I come to a mountain, I fly over it; a precipice, I cross it; a river, I cross it; a storm, I rise above it; a torrent, I skim over it like a bird. I travel without fatigue, and halt without need of rest. I soar above the new cities. I fly with the swiftness of the storm; sometimes near the limit of the air, sometimes a hundred feet above the ground, with the map of Africa unwinding below my eyes in the greatest atlas of the world.'

'He sure makes it sound good,' said enthusiastic Roger. 'By the way, what's that other rope – the one near the valve line?'

'I hope you never have to pull that,' Crosby said. 'It's the rip line. When you pull the valve line you let out just a little gas, slowly. If you pull the rip line, you rip a big hole in the top of the balloon and instantly release all the gas.'

'Why would we ever want to do that?'

'Suppose the worst happens,' said the warden. 'Suppose a storm has caught you and you are being swept along close to the ground at a terrible speed and there are big rocks ahead, or trees, and you are bound to crash into them and be killed unless you do something fast. You pull the rip line. It lets out all the gas, the balloon collapses, the basket drags along the ground for a moment and then stops. You have probably been bruised up a bit, but you're still alive. Of course, you're in a devil of a fix. You may be a hundred miles from the nearest road. You could sew up the rip in the balloon, but you couldn't refill the bag because you haven't any hydrogen. You don't carry cylinders of hydrogen in the basket because the cylinders are too heavy. They are made of steel and each one weighs a ton – they have to be strong because the gas inside is under very high pressure. So there you are with a busted balloon and no gas.'

'What do you do then? Radio for help?'

'The balloon doesn't carry a wireless. Perhaps you walk a hundred miles to the road. Perhaps you stay where you are and spread out the bag in the hope that some search party in a plane will notice it. Whatever you do, your chances are pretty slim. So I hope you never have to pull that rip line.' He grinned. 'Perhaps now that I've told you what can happen you'll think twice about trusting yourselves to a balloon.'

But Hal's reply indicated that he was not too badly frightened. 'How do we get it up to the tracks?'

'That's simple. We'll just moor the trail line to the car and tow it.'

They climbed over the edge. Hal and Mark Crosby went down the ladder. Roger slid down the trail line. He took the rub of the rope on his safari trousers so that his hands were not burned. He reached the ground before the men were halfway down the ladder. They had not seen him pass. When they touched the ground they looked up.

'Where's that kid?' puzzled Hal.

'Just behind you,' said Roger. Hal wheeled about. 'How did you get down so fast?'

'Jumped,' said Roger.

Hal began to untie the trail line from the stump.

'Wait a moment,' said Crosby. 'If you get that thing loose, you'll be carried up out of sight in one minute flat. Let's anchor it first.'

He took the loose end of the rope and fastened it with a slipknot to the rear end of the car. Then while the two boys and the two rangers put their weight on the trail rope Crosby freed it from the stump.

'Let go.' The men let go and the trail line snapped as tight as a bow-string.

'We'll go to the camp first and pick up a few cylinders of gas,' Crosby said.

On the way, the warden asked more questions about the lion hunt.

'What lion did you kill?'

'It was a lioness. She was giving her cub his first lesson in man-eating.'

'Pity to have to kill a female with young.'

'I know. But she jumped me and I had no choice. We're taking care of the cub. We're giving it cow's milk. But it would make a more balanced diet if we could add some cod liver oil, glucose, bonemeal, and a little salt.'

'I can supply all that,' said Crosby. 'How many other

man-eaters do you suppose there are?'

'We've only seen one. But I don't know how one lion could kill so many men.'

'It's quite possible,' the warden said. 'You remember in the history of "the man-eaters of Tsavo" just two man-eaters were responsible for the deaths of more than a hundred men. What sort of lion is this one that you've seen?'

'He's a monster. Grandest lion you ever saw. Nearly a dozen feet long, a good quarter ton, magnificent tawny coat and a coal-black mane. He's as clever as he is big. He appears and disappears like a ghost. The Africans think he's an evil spirit. He seems to kill just for the joy of killing. I wouldn't be surprised if he is the mate of the lioness I shot. He seems bent on taking a terrible revenge for her death. He turns up when we don't expect him and is gone before we can get to him. But the balloon will help. From way up there we ought to be able to spot him long before he gets to the tracks. Then we'll slide down the trail line to our car, drive up the road that runs alongside the railway, and by the time he gets to the tracks we'll be there waiting for him.'

'I hope it works out that way,' said the warden, bringing the car to a stop in the camp.

Men poured out of the cabins and tents to see this strange spectacle – a combination of car and balloon. Some were rangers, some European and American guests. But the ones who really looked good to the boys were their own thirty blacks who had so ably helped them to clear Tsavo of poachers and, before that, had worked so faithfully and fearlessly taking wild animals alive to be shipped to the world's zoos.

There was Toto, Hal's gunbearer, with a grin a yard wide. There was Joro, the chief tracker, and there was brave Mali with his magnificent Alsatian dog, Zulu. Here were all the old friends of many thrilling adventures.

They were full of questions. 'Why do we have to stay here?' 'Why can't we be with you?' 'Why won't King Ku let us help you?'

Hal could only assure them that he and Roger would be back with them soon.

'I think we have only one more man-eater to get,' he said. 'Then our job will be done.'

He didn't say that this one man-eater was equal to a dozen ordinary lions and finishing him off would be no simple matter.

Two extra cylinders of hydrogen were placed in the car and the necessary foods and medicines for the cub.

Then, with a cheerfulness they did not feel, Hal and Roger said goodbye to their friends, checked the trail line to make sure that the balloon was securely hitched to the car, and set out on the twenty-mile trip to the railway camp-ground.

It was necessary to go slowly. Towing a thirty-foot bubble at the end of a hundred-foot line was quite different from towing a vehicle at ground level. The balloon must be kept overhead. If Hal drove fast the balloon would lag behind, lose altitude, and might even drag along the ground. In that case the gas would escape through the hole in the bottom of the bag and the entire envelope would crumple up.

Then there was the wind to reckon with. Luckily the air was reasonably still, but now and then a gust would carry the balloon in front of the car or behind it or cause it to brush against the trees on either side of the road. There was the constant danger that a broken-off branch might puncture the huge bag. Then out would go the gas, and hundreds of yards of nylon would bury the car and the two boys and their hopes.

The first animals they met created no problem. A surprised leopard slunk away into the shadow of the woods. A big-jawed hippo was so intent upon eating a path three feet wide through the grass that it did not notice the balloon over its head. An irritable rhino disturbed by the noise of the engine looked up from his dinner of thorns. But if he saw the balloon at all he probably mistook it for a cloud, since rhinos need glasses.

A little more trouble was caused by a herd of

elephants. They completely blocked the road. Along African roads are posted signs reading, 'Elephants have the right of way.' If there were elephants in the road you did not blow your horn – that would annoy them and invite a charge. You did not flash your lights – that also would be taken by them as an insult. You did not try to push by them – they would push harder than you could and they were quite likely to upset the car and sit on it.

You just turned off your motor and waited. Hal did exactly that. He waited fifteen minutes, a half hour, while Roger grew more and more restless.

The elephants were sucking up dirt from the road and flinging it over their backs. They had found from experience that a coat of dirt was the best protection against biting insects.

'We can't wait here all day,' Roger said. 'Turn on the motor – perhaps that will scare them off.'

'I doubt it,' said Hal. 'But I'll try it.'

He flipped on the ignition. It was the wrong thing to do. The big ears went out, trunks went up, and the leading bull let out a terrific scream. The whole herd began to move towards the car.

Hal slipped the gears into reverse and backed down the road at all the speed the engine would give him. It was not enough. The herd was gaining on him. Just one elephant could smash a car – what would two dozen of them do?

Then help came from the sky. The balloon, which could not travel as fast as the car, trailed lower and lower until it bumped the backs of the elephants.

This tremendous beast has little fear of anything on

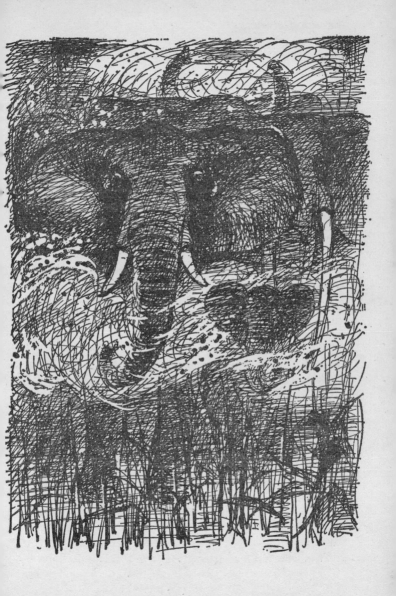

earth. But he is not used to being bombarded from above. With shrill screams of terror the elephants plunged off both sides of the road into the woods.

Hall stopped, then drove forward. The great bag climbed back into the sky.

'A little lower and it would have lost gas,' said Hal, much relieved that the biggest land animal on earth had met its match in something even bigger.

'Good old Jules Verne,' said Roger. 'He came to our rescue just in time.'

9

The devil in Dugan

THE arrival of the balloon in the railway camp created a sensation. Every man stopped work to stare at the great round ball in the sky.

'Now, if we can just find a good anchor,' Hal said.

'How about that log?' said Roger. He pointed out a fallen trunk some fifty feet long. 'That's heavy enough to hold down a dozen balloons. All we have to do is tie our trail line to that.'

Hal grinned. 'You make it sound very simple,' he said. 'But just how do you propose to get the trail line off the car and on to the log?'

'Untie it – then you and I hold the balloon down until we tie up to the log.'

'What makes you think we two can hold it down? Don't forget—there were three of us in that basket and the balloon didn't drop one inch. Just two of us hanging on to a loose trail line would find ourselves in heaven in ten seconds.'

'All right,' Roger said. 'Get eight or ten of the men to hold the balloon down while we tie up to the log.'

'Have you forgotten King Ku's orders – that we must work alone?'

The two sat down on the log and thought. How could

two boys do the work of ten men? It was impossible.
King Ku was asking too much.

Roger raised his head. 'I'm going to try something.'

He went to the car and came back with a length of
rope. He tied one end securely to the trail line and the
other to the log. Then he loosened the trail line from the
car. The balloon bobbed up a few feet but was checked
by the new line. Roger made fast the trail line to the
log.

He stuck out his chest. 'Quite simple,' he said cockily.
'It didn't need your ten men – some brains, that's all.'

Hal smiled. His feelings were a mixture of annoyance
that he had not thought of this simple trick, and pride in
his kid brother who had thought of it.

The boys were eager to climb to the basket and begin
their watch. But there was something Roger wanted to
do first – feed Flop. They took their supplies from the
car and went to the tent. Flop had made himself comfortable in Roger's bed.

Roger, a bit weary, lay down on the bed beside his pet.
Then he came out of the bed like a bolt of lightning. His
neck and cheek were well scratched.

Flop, disturbed in his sleep, had done what all lions
do upon awakening. He had stretched out his legs with
all his claws out, thrusting one paw into Roger's face
and the other into his neck.

Now he opened his eyes wide in an innocent stare,
then waddled up on to his four big feet and demanded
dinner with a loud miaow.

Hal mixed milk with cod liver oil, glucose, bonemeal,
and salt in the proper proportions and Roger fed the
little beast with the help of the bamboo mother.

This time Roger did not bother with disinfectant. The cub's scratches were harmless; he was not yet a meat-eater so there would be no rotting flesh under his claws.

Back to the balloon. Hal and Roger climbed the swaying rope ladder.

The wind had come up and the basket was rolling like a ship in a rough sea. But not quite. At the end of each roll a ship's rail goes down. This basket was more like a hammock. At the end of each swing a hammock goes up. They were being rocked in the cradle of the sky.

But they had been bounced too often in small planes to be bothered by the motion. Equipped with two pairs of binoculars, they began to scan the landscape.

The balloon was at about the middle point of the three-mile stretch of track on which the men were working. The binoculars easily enabled the boys to see a mile and a half in each direction. The country was open savannah, covered with tall tawny grass and punctuated here and there by bushes and termite hills a few feet high.

'Wonderful!' exclaimed Hal. 'Now we're high enough to see behind all those things. If anything stirs in that grass without our spotting it, there's no excuse for us.'

For an hour their binoculars combed the three miles of track and the fairly open country on each side between track and forest. Then Roger nudged his brother. He pointed.

'Look – there. Just coming out of the woods. Four, five, six lions.'

'Let's go,' said Hal. The words were hardly out of his

mouth before he was over the side and sliding down the trail line. Roger followed. In less than twenty seconds they were in the car and speeding down the road that hugged the track. A minute later they tumbled out at the point nearest to the approaching group of lions.

The railway men looked up in surprise. They had been too intent on their work to notice the danger. Hal and Roger snatched two rifles from the car, crossed the track, and walked through the grass towards the lions.

None of the railway men could help them since they were forbidden to carry arms. They went back to their work, glancing anxiously now and then at the boys who were their only protection against six possible man-eaters. The lions came on slowly.

'Perhaps they don't mean any harm,' Roger said. 'How can we tell?'

Hal stripped off his shirt. He went a hundred feet forward and threw down the shirt, then returned to join Roger.

The lions came up to the shirt, sniffed at it curiously, pawed it a little, then went off a short distance and lay down.

'There's your answer,' Hal said. 'There's plenty of man-smell in that shirt. If they had been man-eaters they probably would have ripped it to bits.'

'Not necessarily,' said a voice behind them. They turned to see the white hunter who until now had avoided them.

'I believe your name is Dugan,' said Hal, extending his hand. Dugan shook it, but without enthusiasm. He was a lemon-faced fellow with bitter eyes and a sour twist to the corners of his mouth.

'Just thought you might need a little help,' Dugan said. 'Six lions could be a bit too much for two inexperienced boys.'

Hal smiled. He would not trouble to explain his own long experience with animals. He was not going to let Dugan get his goat.

'You could be wrong about the shirt,' Dugan went on. 'Lions are pretty sly. Perhaps they're just pretending they don't care about man-smell. Perhaps they just want to put you off your guard. Then they'll pounce on you or on one of the men.'

'I know that,' Hal said. 'But we have orders not to kill harmless lions. Since we can't be absolutely sure whether they are harmless or not, let's scare them back into the woods. Let's shoot over their heads. Be very careful,' he said to Roger, 'not to hit one of them. If you do you'll have King Ku and Tanga and the warden and everybody else down on us.'

'Excellent idea,' Dugan said with a mean smile and raised his gun. The three fired at the same instant.

The lions leaped to their feet and made off towards the woods. One lagged behind, and then fell. Hal looked at his brother accusingly.

'You shot him!'

'I did not. I aimed six feet above their heads.'

'Well, if you didn't, who did?' Hal wheeled around to face Dugan.

But Dugan was no longer there. He was running down the tracks towards the station.

The boys remained at their post for a time to be sure that the lions did not return. Then they cautiously approached the one that had fallen. It did not stir. The great golden-haired body was curled up as if in sleep. Blood welled from a bullet hole behind the left ear. It would be a long sleep.

Hal retrieved his shirt. Wearily, they went back to the station to report to Tanga. Hal began to explain, but Tanga cut him short.

'Dugan has already told me about it,' said the station master. 'How could you possibly make such a mistake? Haven't you ever had a gun in your hands before?'

Hal stared. 'You mean – Dugan pinned it on us?'

'Now look here,' Tanga said irritably. 'I don't think too much of Dugan – but at least he knows how to fire a gun. After all, he's a professional hunter. I should have kept him on the job. I was a fool to take on a couple of boys to do a man's work.'

'But listen,' Hal said patiently. 'You are perfectly right about one thing – Dugan knows how to fire a gun.

Doesn't it occur to you that he may have killed that lion on purpose?'

'Why should he do that?'

'To make you think we did it. And apparently he succeeded. You yourself warned us that he would try to do for us. And now when he is doing just that you allow him to get away with it. We let him put one over on us. You are quite right – we are just boys and not very smart. But you, Tanga, you are a man – I never would have thought he could make a fool of *you*.'

The words went home. Tanga writhed in his chair.

'I don't know – I just don't know,' he said confusedly. 'Anyhow I'll have to tell King Ku.'

'Go ahead and tell him,' Hal said. 'There's one good thing about Ku. He's enough of a devil to understand the devil in Dugan.'

10

The tourists and the lion

ONCE again in their basket, the watchmen in the sky had the thrill of being able to see the world and yet not be a part of it.

They were on a planet of their own. Or they were men from Mars in a flying saucer investigating the Earth.

Every detail below stood out sharply – the campground, the roof of the station, the men at work on the tracks, the grassy plain and the woods beyond; to the west, Kilimanjaro raising its snowy head far above the clouds; to the north, the village of Gula on its hilltop; and not far west of it, Mombo village, so plainly visible that you could count the dogs.

In some ways, the balloon had it all over the plane. In a balloon you simply stood still in the sky and had a chance to look. In a plane you shot along at a speed of anywhere from a hundred miles an hour up to heaven knows what and if you saw anything that interested you it was gone before you could get your eyes fixed on it.

In the *Jules Verne* they were only a hundred feet up with a close view of everything. In a small plane they would be riding a mile high, or seven miles high in a jet.

Much of the time there would be a carpet of clouds beneath you hiding the earth. Even if the air were clear the far-away features of the land below would be little more than a blur.

And you would be peering out of a tight little window filmed over with dust or mist, or smudged with grease where the heads of passengers had rested against it. In a few minutes you would give up trying to see anything and would bury yourself in a magazine.

Standing free in an open basket, not cooped in by walls and windows, with a sweeping view on all sides, the idea of reading a magazine was the last thing that would cross your mind.

The train from Mombasa rolled in. Two women stepped out of the train and stood uncertainly on the station platform. Their voices which could not have been heard a hundred feet away on the ground rose easily a hundred feet to the perch in the sky.

'Bless my soul,' said one. 'What a godforsaken place.'

'Wonder how we get a taxi,' said the other.

They approached an African dozing on a bench.

'Pardon me, how do we get to Kitani Safari Lodge?'

The man opened sleepy eyes and waved his hand as if brushing away flies.

'He doesn't understand us. Dear me, what can we do?'

Hal leaned over the edge of the basket. 'I beg your pardon – can I help you?'

The women stared at each other.

'Who said that? Did you hear it?'

'Someone speaking English.'

They looked at the African on the bench. He was asleep. They looked all around.

'I could swear—'

'Don't swear, lady,' Hal said. 'Look up.'

They looked up and gave vent to their astonishment in a little scream.

'Patricia, do you see what I see? A balloon. Of all things!'

'It can't be real.'

'What are you doing up there, young man?'

Hal laughed. 'Just waiting to serve you. What's your trouble?'

'We want to go to Kitani Safari Lodge.'

'I'm afraid you're out of luck for a while. The Lodge car will come to meet the Nairobi train.'

'When will that be?'

'Two hours from now.'

'Two hours! Young man, we're American tourists. We're not used to that kind of service. Two hours indeed! What are we going to do in the meantime?'

'You could sit in the station.'

'We didn't come to Africa to sit in stations. Isn't there anything to see around here?'

'Would you be interested in an African village?'

'Of course.'

'There are two near by. Mombo is just up that path a few minutes' walk.'

'Will you guide us?'

'Sorry, madam, we have a job to do up here. You'll be all right.'

The ladies sputtered a bit over this, looked at their watches, then took the path to Mombo.

The boys watched them as they crossed the open ground, disappeared into a patch of woodland, and appeared again on the other side climbing the small hill to the village.

It was at this moment that Roger saw the lion. It emerged from the woods and followed the two women up the trail. They went on, quite unaware of its presence.

Down the trail rope, like firemen down the pole, slid the two lion-hunters. They snatched rifles from the car and raced across the grassland and through the woods towards the village. Coming out from among the trees they looked anxiously up the path to the hilltop. There was no sign of either ladies or lion.

'Perhaps he's got them already,' Roger gasped.

They puffed their way up the hill and entered the village. They ran between the straw-roofed mud huts and came out into the public dance-ground.

Here there seemed to be great excitement. A chattering mob of villagers was packed tightly around something that must be of great interest to them.

The boys pushed through the crowd to the open space in the centre. There they found both the ladies and the lion.

They leaped in front of the female tourists, prepared to defend them to the death. They levelled their rifles at the possible man-eater. If he made a move towards either the visitors or the villagers, he would pay for it with his life.

The boys rather expected that they would be greeted with cheers and rejoicing because they had arrived just in time to kill a dangerous wild beast. But what they heard was a great swell of angry voices. Then a big black stepped between them and slapped down their guns.

'No, no,' he said. 'You no shoot. If you kill this lion we kill you.'

Hal was puzzled. 'What's so special about this lion?'

The big black fellow, who appeared to be the headman of the village, replied, 'He good lion. He belong
here. Just like dog, only better. He take care of us. If bad
buffalo break in, he kill buffalo. Many forest pigs come,
destroy our garden, he kill pigs.'

The boys looked at each other, shamefaced. They felt
pretty silly. They had come barging in like heroes to
rescue these poor people, only to find that the people
didn't want to be rescued. Even the ladies didn't appre-
ciate their services.

'You don't seem to understand lions very well,' said
the lady named Patricia.

'I suppose you know a good deal about them,' said
Hal politely.

'Yes, we do. We've just been to Kruger – there we
drove around among the lions and they didn't do a thing.
Our guide drove the car up to within fifteen feet of them
and we just sat there and looked at them and they paid
no attention to us. They yawned, and they rolled around
on their backs with their paws in the air just like kittens,
and some of them even went to sleep. They're just dear,
adorable pussycats, that's all.'

'Did you step out of the car?'

'No, that isn't allowed. But I don't see why not. They
were the gentlest, sweetest things – they wouldn't hurt a
fly.'

'I'm afraid you are too trusting,' Hal suggested.

'Don't try to tell me about animals, young man,' said
Patricia tartly. 'I have pussies at home – and these are
just like them. You can see what a darling this one is.'

The 'darling' yawned, displaying fangs three inches
long and as sharp as spears and two rows of ferocious

cutting teeth and grinding molars. Patricia's head would fit very easily in that great terrible mouth.

The village headman apologized to Hal. 'I am sorry if we were rude,' he said. 'It was kind of you to come. You could not know – this is a very unusual lion. Without him to protect us we would have no crops. You have seen our gardens? Come, I will show you.'

They walked to the edge of the village to see the plantings of yams and beans and maize and coffee and fruit. Hal did not need to be told what damage these would suffer if the gardens were invaded by packs of wild pigs, warthogs, rhinos, or baboons. The village was lucky indeed to have such a strong protector.

The people, proud of their crops, had followed to make sure that the boys would see what fine things had been done in the gardens with the help of the tame lion. But the ladies remained behind. They were more interested in the lion itself. The great puss had gone to sleep.

'Now I ask you, Gladys,' said Patricia, 'did you ever see anything more peaceful? Who could be afraid of that?'

'He's sweet,' agreed Gladys. 'I wish we could take away something to remember him by. A teensy-weensy tuft of his mane perhaps.'

'I'll tell you what,' said Patricia enthusiastically. 'Those toe-nails – aren't they the loveliest things? So shiny, just like jewels. If we could get one for you and one for me we could take them to a jeweller and have them set in rings. He wouldn't miss just two toe-nails – anyhow, they'd grow again. I have a pair of scissors in my bag. Shall we try?'

'Why not?' said Gladys.

Fired with this brilliant idea, and armed with the scissors, they crept up to the sleeping pussycat. They lost a little of their nerve as they came close, for the great bushy head made them feel small by comparison. Should they change their minds? Patricia looked at Gladys and Gladys looked at Patricia. It didn't seem like quite such a good idea now.

But wouldn't it be wonderful to show the folks back home a ring on your finger with a huge glossy jewel and have them ask, 'What is it?' And you reply, 'A lion's toenail. I cut it off his claw myself.' And they would say, 'A dead lion?' And you would say, 'No, a live one.' And they would say, 'Ooooo, how brave you are!' And you would say, 'It was nothing. They are just big pussycats, you know.'

Patricia, trying to keep her hand steady, brought the scissors close to a lovely nail. The great beast's breath was hot on her face. She got the claw between the scissor blades. She tried to cut, but the nail was tough. She exerted a little more pressure.

Hal and Roger, returning, saw this strange spectacle – two women on their knees trying to cut off the claws of the King of Beasts. Hal dared not shout for fear of waking the lion. He waved his arms in warning but they were not looking his way.

The lion, slightly disturbed, opened one sleepy eye. He didn't quite like what he saw and with one swing of his giant paw he swept both ladies head over heels across the stony ground to end up in a heap against a mud wall.

The lion closed his eye and went back to sleep.

Hal and his brother helped the ladies to their feet. Their faces were scratched by the stony ground, their dresses were soiled and torn. Their nerves were badly shaken. They sat down weakly on the edge of the hollowed log that served the village as a signal drum. They looked reproachfully at the sleeping lion.

'Now how could he do a thing like that!' complained Patricia.

Hal sat down beside them. He didn't like to lecture but if somebody didn't set these ladies straight they were very apt to be killed.

'I'm sorry for what happened,' he said. 'But it really wasn't the lion's fault. Suppose you woke to find someone attacking you with a pair of scissors. Wouldn't you do something about it?'

'But the lions we've seen have been so gentle.'

'They're gentle so long as you leave them alone. But remember, the lion is the most dangerous animal in Africa.'

'Oh now, aren't you exaggerating?'

'I don't think so. I'm just telling you what the great hunters and naturalists say. Records show more fatal accidents from lions than from any other animal. The famous hunter, Selous, thought the lion the most dangerous of all African big game. The two white hunters, Tarlton and Cunningham, put the lion at the top of the list. Game Warden Temple-Perkins, after thirty years of experience, graded the dangerous animals by points. Most of them ranked less than a hundred. The buffalo and elephant each got five hundred and fifty points. He gave the lion seven hundred and twenty-five points as the most dangerous of all.'

'That's not the way I heard it,' objected Gladys. 'I've read articles by tourists – they didn't have the least trouble with lions. They debunked them – said they were much over-rated.'

'Do you know why?' Hal replied. 'They saw the lions just as you did – from a car. They didn't get out of the car. If they had, they might tell a different story. You can't debunk the lion. How do you suppose he got the title of King of Beasts? He has always been the symbol of courage. King Richard was proud to be called "Richard the Lion-Heart". The kings of England and Scotland displayed lions on their shields. The rulers of Norway, Denmark, and Holland, all had lions on their coats-of-arms. In Egypt lions were worshipped as gods. The priests bathed them in perfumed water and fed them the choicest food and entertained them with sacred music. They were embalmed like humans when they died and they were buried with great ceremony. Even today all through Africa men are proud to be called lions. The Emperor Haile Selassie calls himself "The Lion of Judah". The elephant is a great animal too. But did you ever hear of a king calling himself an elephant? Or a rhino or buffalo or giraffe? You can't imagine Richard wanting to be called "Richard the Hippo-Heart". No, it's always the lion. The Emperor keeps a tame lion in his palace. Chiefs in the Congo wear lion skins to show that they are great men. Many tribes worship a lion-god.'

'Why do they think the lion is so wonderful?'

'I suppose because the lion is brave. You said yourself the lions don't move away when you drive up. They aren't afraid of you. They know they are stronger than

you are. You felt what just one little tap of one paw
could do. If he had really swatted you, you would not be
alive now. I saw two lions drag a dead horse up a steep
hill. Twenty men couldn't have done it. A lion can jump
over a fence twelve feet high and climb out again dragging a cow heavier than himself. A lion is afraid of a
man with a gun – but not of any man without one. He's
not afraid of any animal on earth – except the ant. A
swarm of ants chewing into his hide makes him very
unhappy. Most people think lions can't climb trees.
Usually they don't, but I saw one climb thirty feet high
to get a gazelle put there by a leopard. It's hard to kill a
lion. He doesn't know when he's dead. A white hunter
tells of one lion that ran twenty yards with a bullet in his
heart. Many a hunter has been killed because the lion
kept right on coming after it had been fatally shot.'

'All right,' said Gladys. 'We'll admit the lion is strong.
But there's something more important than that. Is he
intelligent? He looks so sleepy and stupid.'

'He's not stupid. He's so smart he can make plans, like
a human being. For instance, suppose there's a kraal or
corral full of cattle. Suppose the lions are hungry and
want one of those cattle. But the fence around the kraal
is too high for them to jump over. Now, put your human
brain to work on that. If you were a lion, how would you
get one of those cattle if you couldn't get into the kraal?'

The ladies gave it some thought, and shook their
heads. 'Too deep for me,' said Gladys.

'The lions plan it this way. Most of them stay on one
side of the kraal and make no sound. Two or three go on
the other side and set up a terrific roaring. There's nothing that terrifies cattle more than the roar of lions. The

frightened cattle stampede away from the sound across the kraal and crash into the fence with such force that they break it down. They rush out among the waiting lions who leap on their backs and break their necks.'

'That's pretty smart,' admitted Patricia. 'But lions have such horrible habits. Some of them are cannibals.'

'They're not cannibals,' Hal protested. 'A cannibal is one who eats others of its own kind. A hyena is a cannibal. He will eat another hyena. But a lion will not eat another lion unless he is starving.'

'They do worse than that,' said Patricia. 'Some of them are man-eaters.'

Hal nodded. 'I know. We're after one now. But we don't despise him because he's a man-eater. After all, you and I are animal-eaters. But we don't think we're so horrible because we kill and eat cattle and sheep and pigs and wild game. We can sit down to a meal of roast beef without any guilty feeling whatever. And the lion has no reason to feel guilty when he eats that animal called man. Of course we must stop him, but we can't blame him.'

'But there are so many other animals to eat – why can't they be satisfied with them?'

'Lions do eat other animals when they can catch them. In fact most lions would rather have the meat of other animals, not man-meat. They don't like the smell of man. But when a lion's leg is crippled by a bullet or a spear he can't run fast enough to overtake most animals. In that case, the hunter who crippled him is to blame. Or perhaps the lion has been badly hurt in a fight with an elephant or rhino. Or he may just be too old to hunt fast game. Or, as often happens, a porcupine has backed into his face and left a lot of painful quills sticking in him. The mango fly lays eggs in the quill-wounds and the eggs turn into masses of worms all around the mouth and eyes. The pain is terrible, the beast becomes irritable and savage, he can't see well enough to hunt, it's too painful for him to eat tough meat, so he overcomes his dislike for human flesh and starts eating that because it is soft and because humans are easy to catch. A human being without a gun is a very helpless creature. He can't run as fast as other animals. His sense of hearing is not as good, nor his sense of smell, nor his sense of sight. He doesn't have horns like an antelope nor the tusks of the warthog and he can't kick like a giraffe. So it's quite natural for the starving lion to take the easy way out and begin eating humans. The worst of it is that a man-eater teaches its cubs to be man-eaters and so the habit is passed on from one generation to the next. Of course this has to be stopped and that's what we're doing right now – trying to track down a lion that has been killing the men working on the tracks. And we'd better get back to our job. Will you go with us down to the station?'

They had not been away from their post for more than a half-hour. Yet in that short time two more men had been taken.

Tanga waited near the balloon to tell them the news.

'Where were you?' he demanded angrily.

'Mombo village. We saw a lion going there – thought it might be a man-eater. But it turned out to be their protector.'

'You didn't shoot it?'

'Of course not.'

'If you had, the whole village would be down on you.'

'But this killing – how did it happen?'

'The lion sneaked up through the grass. Nobody saw it coming. It grabbed one man and made off with him. The man's buddy attacked the lion with a crowbar. The lion knocked it out of his hands, leaped on him and broke his neck. He died instantly. Then the lion killed the other man and dragged him off into the woods.'

'What kind of lion was it?'

'A very large male with a black mane.'

'I'm sorry we weren't here,' Hal said. 'But when we saw the lion on the way to the village we felt we had to do something about it.'

'I can understand that,' Tanga admitted. 'But I must say you are having a streak of very bad luck.'

He went back to the station, shaking his head.

11

Tin pans and elephants

WALKING with head bowed, Tanga almost collided with a tall young black. He looked up and recognized Basa of the village of Gula.

Basa had not yet noticed him. His gaze was fixed upon the basket a hundred feet above. The boys were just climbing into it.

A terrible hate was stamped on Basa's face. If a look could kill, Hal and Roger would have fallen dead at that instant. Basa held a bow and on his back was a quiver of arrows. The dark brown stains on the shafts showed that the arrows were poisoned. The boys, confined to the basket, were sitting ducks for those arrows. But Tanga could not believe that the handsome young Negro was thinking of murder.

But he smelled trouble. It was part of his job to avoid trouble. There were no police in this area. The station master was the only public official except for the district officer, King Ku. If there was any violence brewing in this young man's mind Tanga should know about it.

'Good morning, Basa. You look as if you didn't like our white friends.'

Basa saw him for the first time. He mumbled a reply and started to move away.

'Wait a minute,' said Tanga. 'Is anything wrong?'

Basa stared at him bitterly. 'You ask me that? You know what happened.'

'What do you mean?'

'My father. You know he was killed.'

'Yes. A lion with a black mane killed him.'

'No. It was those two.' He pointed aloft. 'They killed him.'

'How do you make that out?'

'The lion entered their tent. It was an easy shot. They could have killed it. They let it get away. It went into the next tent and got my father. They were to blame. They killed my father.'

'Oh, come now,' said Tanga. 'You're letting your hate run away with you. Their revolver was knocked out of reach. They did the best they could.'

'With pancake flour?' said Basa sarcastically. 'What a way to fight a lion. No excuse you can make for them is good enough. Their neglect and stupidity killed my father. And they will have to pay for it.'

Tanga laid his hand on the young man's arm. 'Basa, listen to reason. If you think you have any case against them, take it to court. Don't appoint yourself judge and executioner.'

'Court!' sneered Basa. 'You know very well that is not the way of our tribe. If a man is killed, his son must avenge his death. He cannot leave it to any court or judge or jury. He must do it himself. And if you have any respect for the customs of our people, you will not interfere.'

'I respect your customs,' Tanga said. 'But let me warn you, if you make one move to carry out your threat I'll put the handcuffs on you myself and you will be on your way to the Nairobi jail. Think it over. And try to change your mind about these boys.'

'Why should I change my mind?'

'I'll give you a good reason. Did you realize that if it hadn't been for Hal Hunt your father's body would have been eaten by hyenas and jackals? His skeleton would be lying there now if Hunt had not come and told you what had happened. He made it possible for you to give your father a proper burial in your own village. Think about that. And remember that you have been educated. You belong to the new world of justice, not to the old world of vengeance. Now go, and don't let me hear any more about this.'

Muttering angrily, Basa turned on his heel and strode off towards the village of Gula.

A strong wind had come up. The *Jules Verne* was tugging at its trail line. The basket bounced under the feet of the two lion scouts. The dangling rope ladder whipped back and forth like the tail of a tiger. It was dangerous to stay up – it would be dangerous to go down. Anyone tossing back and forth on that ladder might lose his grip and be dashed on the stones below.

Roger looked up at long black fingers of cloud clutching at the great bag.

'Should we go down or stick it out?'

'Six of one and half a dozen of the other,' said Hal. 'Look at those animals.'

The change in the weather had electrified everything that could move. A herd of zebras ran at full speed

across the veld for no apparent good reason. Impalas
that seemed to have wings in their heels soared over ant-
hills ten feet high. The excited screaming of baboons
came down the wind from the forest a quarter of a mile
away. Lions that had been sleeping in the sun were
roused by the chilling wind and began prowling about
restlessly. The boys kept their binoculars trained on
them – they might or might not be man-eaters.

'Elephants!' exclaimed Roger.

A herd of forty or fifty of the great beasts was charging up the hill towards the village of Gula. Like a ty-
phoon they swept in among the mud huts, not troubling
to go around them, but plunging through and over them,
flattening them to the ground as if they were castles of
sand. Men and women came shrieking from the huts.

'Come on!' said Hal and slid down the trail line
promptly followed by Roger. Hal led the way at a run to
the station.

'Tanga,' he panted. 'Elephants raiding Gula. Send up
your men – with pans.'

Then he and Roger raced to the village. Tanga acted
promptly, and within a minute railway men began to
stream up the path, each armed with a weapon that elephants keenly dislike – a tin pan.

They found the villagers running about aimlessly like
ants whose nest has been disturbed. The elephants were
now in the village gardens, rooting up and devouring the
vegetables, tearing down the coffee and fruit trees, eating
and destroying, trampling with their great feet the crops
that meant the difference between life and death for the
village.

Hal hastily took command of the men, lining them up

side by side, then ordering them forward like an army, each one hammering on his pan with a stick or stone or his knuckles if he had nothing better.

The combined din was terrific and rose even above the trumpeting of the elephants. The men of the village joined in, banging on native drums.

They were so occupied when Black Mane came on the scene. The wise old man-eater knew very well how to let elephants do a part of his work for him. When a man-eater sees a herd marching towards a village he falls in behind it. The men of the village rush out to drive away the elephants and are so busy they do not notice the skulking lion. The man-eater is then free to seize anyone who has been left behind.

In a hut at the edge of the village a woman bent over a cooking-fire. Her husband had gone to join the fight against the elephants. In his haste he had not quite closed the door. The woman's father, old and ill, lay on a straw mat.

Silently, Black Mane pushed open the door, passed across the room, and fastened his jaws upon the ribs of the helpless man. The first the woman knew of it was when her father cried, 'Lion's got me.'

She turned to see her father being dragged off the mat by the enormous lion. She was a brave woman. She tore a burning log from the fire and struck the lion in the face.

Black Mane was not used to being treated in this way, especially by a woman. The flying sparks burned his eyes and the smoke made him sneeze. He dropped the man, sat back on his haunches, and looked at the woman with surprise as much as to say, 'Don't you know you're only a woman? You're not supposed to act like that. You're supposed to scream and run away.'

Her unexpected attack had made him forget the man. With his eyes still smarting painfully, he walked out of the hut. He would try again somewhere else.

The woman ran to her father. His eyes were closed. She spoke to him but he did not answer. The great fangs had reached his heart. She gathered him in her arms and wept.

So the men found her when they returned after driving out the elephants. And they saw Black Mane scratching at the door of another hut. They called on the official lion-killers, Hal and Roger, the only men who carried guns.

Not quite the only ones. There was also Dugan who had been attracted to the scene by the trumpeting of the elephants and the thunder of pans and drums.

Hal motioned the men to stay back and keep quiet. He and Roger crept towards Black Mane, still scratching at the door. They must get near enough for a really deadly shot.

Dugan stood by the village headman and watched. 'They'll never do it,' he said. 'They don't know one end of a gun from the other.'

'How about you?' the headman said. 'Can't you do it for us?'

'Of course I could. But it's not my job.'

'It was your job, until they came.'

Yes, thought Dugan, it was my job until those two babes in the woods took it away from me. Here's my chance. If I kill that lion, Tanga will get rid of these children and take me back. He drew his revolver.

'Don't you need to get closer?' said the headman.

'Nonsense. I can do it from here.' He raised his gun and fired.

Black Mane, alarmed by the report, and feeling the swish of the bullet through the hair on the back of his neck, bounded away. Hal and Roger fired instantly but the great animal was already behind an ant-hill and when he could be seen again he was well on his way to the forest, proceeding at a speed almost equal to that of a cheetah.

A groan of disappointment rose from the railway workers and the men of Gula. A wailing sound came from the hut where a woman held her father's body in her arms.

'Doggone that Dugan!' said Roger. 'If he hadn't interfered that lion would be dead by now. Where is that son of a gun? We ought to have it out with him.'

But Dugan, ashamed of his failure to hit a standing target, had again done his famous vanishing act.

The railway men were streaming down the hill to their job. The villagers were chattering excitedly.

'What are they saying?' Hal asked the headman.

'They say you will never kill that lion. It is not really a lion. It is a wizard that has turned himself into a lion. It has a lion's body but a man's brain. We know much about these things in Africa. We know that a man who is dead and buried can dig his way out of the soil and become a lion. We know that a witch doctor can turn a stick into a lion and it will kill and then turn back into a stick. We hear lions talking together in real man-language. We know that a bullet turns to water when it strikes a witch-lion. We know that in a village of three hundred people beyond that mountain the chief died and became a lion and began to kill and eat the people. They had to abandon their village, burn it to the ground, and move to another place far away. We know there is great magic in the lion. A charm made of his claws makes you bullet-proof. If you tie it around your leg it gives you great speed. A collar made of his neck-bones brings you luck. A necklace made of his whiskers is rich in magic. If you eat his eyes you can see better. If you eat a lion's heart you will have great courage. The lion who kills men has strong magic. I know the white man has magic and I hoped yours would be stronger than the lion's. How ignorant I was!'

And how ignorant you are, thought Hal. The headman of a village should be leading his people up into the light, instead of which this man was stumbling along with them in the dark.

'Is there a school in Gula?' Hal asked.

'No school. Why should we have a school? We have the wisdom of our fathers and of their fathers.'

Hal's eyes swept over the village. Even the huts that had not been trampled by the elephants were poor things of mud and straw. How little had been accomplished by the wisdom of all the fathers. His heart went out to these people. They were as good stuff as could be found anywhere, but they needed education and opportunity. And what a sad mess they were in now – with half of their huts ruined and about a third of the gardens destroyed. At least he had been able with the help of the railway men to save the place from total destruction – but he had not prevented Black Mane from taking another victim.

12

The knife

ON the way back to the balloon, Hal and Roger had to
go through the patch of woodland.

As they walked through the half-dark of the big trees,
they heard the rustle of bare feet in the leaves behind
them. They turned to face Basa.

This time the powerful young black carried no bow
and arrow. Hal hoped it meant that Basa had decided to
be more friendly. His hope was dashed when Basa drew
a murderous-looking long-bladed bush-knife from its
sheath.

'Now I have you where I want you,' he said with a
sinister smile. 'No one will disturb us here. Now you will
pay.'

'Basa,' Hal said, 'can't we forget all this and be
friends? We are sorry for what happened to your father,
but we were not to blame.'

'You killed him,' Basa retorted. 'And then there is
what happened today. You allowed your lion to kill
another of our men.'

'What do you mean, our lion?' put in Roger hotly.
'You talk as if we sent him.'

'The man who was killed was one of the chief elders of
our village. It was your job to protect him and all others
from man-eaters.'

Roger was about to reply angrily but Hal checked him. 'No use losing our tempers,' he said. 'Basa, there is truth in what you say. So far we have failed to catch the black-maned one. But we have done what we could. Didn't we come this morning to help you drive out the elephants?'

'Yes, you saved a few cabbages and yams. But what are they compared with a man's life? Enough talk. Defend yourself.'

'One more word before you do something foolish,' said Hal. 'Do I have to remind you that we have guns?'

'I know you have guns,' Basa said contemptuously. 'White men are cowards – they are afraid to fight without guns. As for me, this will do.' A ray of sun through the trees struck his two-foot blade and made it glow like fire.

Hal gave up. The only way to get sense into this young hothead was to beat it in. He wasn't sure he could do it, but he would have to give it a try. He took out his revolver and dropped it into the grass. Roger took out his gun and held on to it.

'Drop it,' Hal said. 'And keep out of this.' Roger dropped his gun.

Basa, though surprised to see his enemies get rid of their weapons just before a fight, showed no inclination to give up his own. He leaped forward and slashed with such power that this blow alone could have separated head from body if Hal had not ducked.

The knife had not yet completed its swing before Hal's right fist went up to the black man's chin and his left went straight for his solar plexus.

This double play should have staggered any ordinary

man, but Basa was not ordinary. He came on again with a downsweep of his blade that should split a head in two. Hal was not there when it arrived. With a sidelong movement he seized his enemy's sword arm and gave it a twist that loosened the fingers and sent the knife spinning. It barely escaped Roger and drove its point deep into a tree.

Basa did not seem worried by the loss of his knife. His heavy fists battered Hal's face. In a slugging match Hal saw that he had no chance against the big black.

He turned a boxing bout into a wrestling match. Now it was a question of skill, not just brute strength. He had never learned much judo or karate, but enough to know how to flip his opponent over his head and lay him flat on the ground, face down.

This he did. And before the astonished Basa could recover from his surprise, Hal sat down on him with such force that he completely drove the wind out of his lungs. Nevertheless Basa struggled to get up. Hal brought down his open hand edge first on the spine at that vulnerable point between neck and head. Basa blacked out.

When he came to fifteen minutes later he found his hands and feet securely tied with that natural rope of the African forest, the liana. Hal still sat on his back.

'Go ahead,' Basa mumbled, his mouth in the dust. 'Get it over with.'

'What are you talking about?'

'Kill me.'

'I have no desire to kill you.'

'I want to kill *you*. And I'll do it if I live.'

'You'll think better of it,' Hal guessed. 'I've been waiting for you to come around because I want to talk to you.'

'The time for talk is past. There's nothing but killing now.'

'Sorry to disappoint you,' Hal said. 'But there's not going to be any killing. I'm going to sit right here until you tell me what's really eating you. It can't be this old revenge stuff. You're too intelligent for that. There must be something else that's bothering you. What is it?'

'Nothing else.'

'All right, I'll just sit here until you think of something.'

'Sit as long as you please.'

But after another half hour Basa grew restless. 'How long are you going to keep this up?'

'Until you tell me what makes you such a sourpuss.'

'What's it to you?'

'Just could be that I could help you shake it off.'

'What are you, a missionary or something?'

'Far from it. But I happen to like you – you bloody brute – and I think you're being wasted. Come clean. What's back of all this? How can such a young fellow be such an old grouch? You don't want me dead. What is it you really want?'

Basa lay quiet a few minutes. Then he laughed weakly. 'You're a mind reader.'

'How so?'

'I never really wanted to kill you. It was something else. Let me up and I'll tell you about it.'

Hal began to untie the lianas. 'Don't,' cried Roger. 'He's just trying to trick you.'

'I think not,' said Hal. He unbound Basa's hands and

feet. Basa stiffly got up. His bush-knife was within reach but he made no attempt to get it. He sat down on a log.

'I don't know what to make of you,' he said. 'You had your chance to do me in. And I deserved it. I've been a crab for a long time. I took it out on my father while he was alive – then on you. I've been hating everybody.'

'That's a strange attitude for anyone who's had your advantages. You've been to school.'

'That's just it,' said Basa. 'I've been to school. I thought it would open the doors for me. I thought I could do big things for my village.'

'What big things?'

'I wanted to be a teacher. What my village needs most is a school. I went to King Ku about it. He laughed at me. I went to the Board of Education in Nairobi. They said our children could walk to school in Halo fifty miles away. I told them that was like saying they could go to school on the moon. They said they couldn't hire more teachers. I said I would work without pay. They said they had no funds to build a school. I said our village could build it. They said they had no money for maintenance, for books, pencils, paper, blackboards, and all that. They told me to forget it. I thought I might go ahead alone because my father was earning a little working on the railway. Now he is dead and I must work to feed the family. I applied for a job on the tracks but they told me they are laying off men and don't need me.'

'It's just as well,' said Hal. 'With your education you should be able to get something better than a pick-and-shovel job on the tracks.'

'So now I'm at loose ends,' said Basa. 'And I'm pretty

sore about it. What was the use of all that stuff at school if I can't do anything with it?'

'You could get something in Nairobi.'

'I suppose I could. But it's a funny thing – I've always dreamed of doing something for my own people. That's what was in the back of my head all the time I was in school. Nairobi doesn't need me. Gula does. And here I am just the way you had me ten minutes ago – bound hand and foot.'

'Well, I untied you, didn't I?' Hal said. 'And now I'll untie you again. I know what my father would say if he had heard your story. So I'll say it for him. We have thirty men who are just itching for something to do. I'll send them up to help the men of Gula build your school.

And the Hunt family will be proud to maintain it and pay the teacher.'

Basa's mouth dropped open and his eyes became big and round. He turned his head slowly and gazed for a full minute at Hal as if he had never seen him before. Then he mumbled: 'I – I don't know what to say.'

'Then say nothing. How soon could you begin?'

'Any time. Tomorrow morning.'

'You don't need time to make plans?'

'Plans! I've been planning it for years.'

'Okay. I'll phone the Lodge as soon as I get back to the station. My men will be on hand tomorrow morning. As soon as you get them started, you can hop the train to Nairobi and order the desks and benches and books and blackboards and everything else you need. Have them send the bill to me.'

Basa began to believe that this crazy white man really meant what he was saying. The sun broke through the thundercloud of his face. His eyes crinkled at the corners and a grin spread from ear to ear. Hal had never seen Basa smile before and he thought he had never seen any-one more handsome.

'I go to tell my people,' Basa said, and started up the path.

'Wait,' Hal said. 'Aren't you forgetting something?'

Hal drew the knife from the tree and handed it to Basa. Basa grinned again. He thrust the knife into its sheath and took off at a run towards Gula.

13

Flight of the 'Jules Verne'

AFTER telephoning, the Hunts went back to their tent, hastily fed Flop and themselves, then started for the balloon.

'There's King Ku,' said Roger. The big black district officer was inspecting the work on the tracks.

'We'll speak to him,' Hal suggested. Ku saw them approaching and deliberately walked away.

'No soap,' Hal said regretfully. 'I'd like to know why he's down on everyone with a white skin.'

The *Jules Verne* was doing a weird dance in the strong wind. The basket was leaping like a gazelle. It certainly was not a good day for ballooning, but the boys had no choice. The rope ladder was thrashing back and forth. Hal caught it and they began to climb. It was like climbing a snake. The ladder twisted and squirmed like something alive.

Breathless, they reached the basket and climbed in. It was not easy to hang on with one hand and manipulate the binoculars with the other. What they saw was indistinct because of the jiggling of the glasses. The tall, lion-coloured grass billowing under the wind might be just grass or it might be lions. They soon became dizzy with looking and queasy at the stomach from the constant leaping and swooping of their magic carpet.

But they stayed at their posts until dark. Then, when the last trackmen had returned to camp, they prepared to come down.

Hal threw one leg over the basket edge and laid hold of the trail rope. It didn't feel right. Usually it was tight and taut. Now it was limp in his hands.

And he was suddenly conscious of a new feeling of motion. The wind was not rushing by them now. Instead, they seemed to be going with the wind.

It was true. The ground was slipping backward beneath them. The trail line must have come loose – or had someone cut it? He could dimly see the black shadow of a man moving away from the spot where the balloon had been moored.

He drew his leg back into the basket and said as calmly as he could, 'Guess we're going to take a ride.'

Roger looked down to see the roof of the station scudding by beneath.

'Holy smoke!' he exclaimed. 'Let's slide down the trail rope while there's still time.'

'And lose the balloon? Heaven knows where it may smash up.'

'I'd rather not be in it when it does,' Roger said fervently. 'Can't we do something? How about pulling the valve line? That will let out some gas and the balloon will settle down.'

'And tear itself to pieces on the trees,' Hal guessed. 'And smash us to bits at the same time. We must be almost up to the trees already.'

He snatched the flashlight from its bracket and played it downwards. Its light did not reach the ground. He turned it off and put it back. The roof of the station had

been white and therefore visible. But now in the gathering darkness everything below was blotted out.

'Doesn't seem as if we're moving at all,' Roger said.

While they had been anchored they had been forced to shout to make themselves heard above the roar of the wind through the rigging and around the great ball. Now there was complete silence.

'That's because we're riding the wind, not resisting it,' Hal said. 'But we're not standing still. That was a forty-mile-an-hour wind. That means we're shooting along at forty miles an hour at this very minute.'

The silence was now broken by a rushing sound ahead.

'Quick!' said Hal. 'Sandbags out.'

'What *is* that sound?' said Roger as they began throwing out sand.

'Wind in the trees. If we can get enough sand out in a hurry we may rise above them. If we strike them, it's all up.'

Hal flashed a light on the altimeter.

'We're only a hundred and ten feet up – that's not good enough. Some of these kapoks top a hundred and fifty.' More sand went over the side.

The whoosh of the wind tearing at branches and leaves told them they had almost arrived. The balloon was rising, but slowly. They could not possibly reach a hundred and fifty in time.

Roger kept throwing out sand. Hal was hauling up the rope ladder. It must not be allowed to get tangled in the branches. The trail line should come up too, but there was no time for that.

Then they struck. The impact nearly threw them out

of the basket. Leaves and twigs thrashed into their faces. Now that they were no longer moving with the wind, they felt the full force of it.

Would branches puncture the bag? Hal directed his light up. No, the bag was above the treetops. Only the basket had struck.

'What do we do now?' came from Roger. 'Climb out?'

Hal circled the light outside the basket.

'Not a branch strong enough to hold a monkey.'

'Gee, that's bad.'

'No, that's good. If nothing big is holding us we may pull free.'

Vain hope. Another gust drove the basket deeper into the tree. Hornbills disturbed in their nests flew off with a great whoop and holler. This bird utters its cries through a hollow nose-chamber that makes every squeak come out like a blast of a bassoon. This did nothing for the boys' nerves.

A more powerful burst of wind sent the basket scraping and shuddering through the treetop. Hal had been pulling in the trail line. Now it had caught on something and stubbornly refused to let loose. He exerted all his strength but without effect.

What he could not do the wind did for him. A stronger blast than ever struck the great forty-foot bag and tore the basket and the trail line out of the clutching grasp of the big tree.

They were once more riding the wind and were able to finish pulling in the trail line. Roger shouted with joy. It seemed for a moment as if all their troubles were over. Now all they had to do was to select a nice smooth spot without trees, let out some gas, and come down.

But it was not to be so simple. If there was any smooth spot without trees, they had no way of seeing it. And away from the railway there was not likely to be such a spot. And a landing in this wind would mean that the basket would be dragged hundreds of feet over rough ground, dashed against cement-hard ant-hills and big rocks, and both basket and boys would probably be ground into mincemeat.

Or they might come down into a surprised herd of elephants or irritable rhinos, or hungry hyenas. Lions too were on the prowl at this time of night.

Every minute was taking them farther away from camp. But how about that other camp, the Kitani Safari Lodge? This was an east wind. Hal figured it should be carrying them almost straight west along the valley of the Tsavo River and perhaps over the Lodge itself.

They might already be above the cabins and tents of the Lodge. He turned his flashlight on the great bag over his head. He desperately hoped they would see it. But he knew in his heart that the chances were a hundred to one against it. The warden and his rangers and guests did not make a practice of wandering around outside after nightfall when wild animals made a parade ground of the camp.

But he kept his light on the bag. Then he saw a glimmer below. That was light shining from cabin windows.

'Shout,' he said to Roger. They shouted loud enough to wake the dead. Their shouts were carried away on the wind. In ten seconds they were swept beyond the camp and over some of the wildest country of East Africa. There was now nothing but blackness below.

And blackness ahead. It loomed into the sky, shutting off the stars. Away at the top of this great tower of blackness was something white, like a white roof, or a white cloud in the night sky.

What could it be, this black tower with a white roof? Hal tried to reconstruct the map in his imagination. What was the country like straight west of Kitani?

Then it came to him. The mountain!

His heart skipped a beat. He tried to keep his voice calm. 'I'm afraid we're in for a bad time. Kilimanjaro – straight ahead. We're bound to smash into it.'

Roger peered at the black monster with the cap of white.

'Can't we go around it?'

'No chance. You're not in an aeroplane. No way to steer this thing.'

'How about going over it?'

'Nineteen thousand feet high. The highest mountain in all Africa. We might leap-frog over a six-thousand-foot peak. But even if we threw out every ounce of sand I don't see how we could climb to nineteen thousand.'

'Well, if we do strike it,' said Roger, 'perhaps we'll get off with a few bruises. Then we can walk down the slope and find a village.'

Hal laughed bitterly. 'Slope, the man says. What slope? Don't you remember how this side of the mountain looks through your binoculars? A straight up-and-down cliff of solid rock. When we crash, don't try to get out of the basket. There'll be nothing to get out on. If the balloon holds its gas, and if we aren't knocked into the next world by the blow, we may stick there until we...'

'Until we starve?'

'Until the wind changes and blows us off.'

'That's not likely,' Roger said. 'You know this is a trade wind.'

'Right – and it blows pretty steadily from east to west most of the year. Still, miracles do happen. Let's hope for one.'

Hal had a scientific mind, but in the excitement of the moment he could hardly be expected to remember all the laws of nature. Roger beamed a flashlight ahead. The cliff could be plainly seen. But the *Jules Verne* was not approaching it at forty miles an hour.

'We're slowing down,' Roger said. 'How could that be?'

Hal guessed the reason. 'The cliff blocks the wind so perhaps we'll strike without having the breath knocked out of us.'

But they did not strike. Instead, the cliff began to slide down before their eyes. Or so it seemed. It took a moment to realize that it was not the cliff that was dropping but the balloon that was going up. Why should it suddenly start to climb?

Hal looked at the altimeter. Five hundred feet, a thousand, fifteen hundred, two thousand. It made the head a bit dizzy. Five thousand, ten thousand, fifteen thousand.

'We're caught in a thermal,' Hal said.

'Just what is a thermal?'

'Rising body of hot air.'

'But why should there be hot air here?'

'The cliff. It has stored up the sun's heat. The hot rock warms the air. Hot air rises, so up we go with it.'

'Not a bad miracle,' said Roger gratefully.

So the wind had not died down after all. Striking the rock, it was forced to go somewhere. A good part of it decided to go up, helped by the heat of the precipice.

'I only hope it continues,' Hal said.

'Why shouldn't it?'

'We're getting up into colder air. It's like going from the equator to the arctic. Half an hour ago, tropical jungle. And now look.'

The heated rock had given way to ice and snow. In the arms of the dying thermal the balloon struggled over a glacier that never died. The *Jules Verne* began to sink.

'Out with some sand,' cried Hal. 'If we get stranded here we'll freeze to death.'

The shower of sandbags did not help much. The basket began to drag over the snow-banks. Fresh snow was falling and the wind was biting cold.

Roger tried to cheer himself and his brother by saying, 'Well, we can build an igloo and live up here until help comes.' He shivered. His finger-tips were already freezing and he was suffering from lack of oxygen.

The basket stumbled and stopped. A gust of wind carried it a little farther, then it stopped again. Out with more sand. Struggling painfully, like a man limping, the basket hobbled over the snow-banks – then suddenly took heart and rose a few feet. The air seemed warmer than before. Below, dimly seen through the snow-storm, was no snow or ice, but a large black hole. Far down in it was the gleam of fire.

Some tens of thousands of years ago Kilimanjaro had been an active volcano. Recently new signs of activity had been reported. There was no spouting of lava and no disappearance of snow and ice, but one of the many craters had begun to steam.

It was just enough to save the *Jules Verne*. It rose gently to some fifty or sixty feet and presently it was across the top.

The boys breathed again. 'I'll bet it's the first time anybody ever climbed that mountain in a basket,' Roger said.

14

The field of swords

THE balloon began to fall.

Roger noticed it first. 'Seems to me as if everything's dropping out from under us.'

Hal looked at the altimeter. It read eighteen thousand feet. Even as he kept his light on it, it slid down to seventeen, sixteen, fifteen thousand.

'It was bound to happen,' Hal said. 'The hot thermal that carried us up got chilled by the glaciers and snowbanks and snow-storm while it was passing over the mountain-top. Now it's cold air, and of course cold air falls.'

This side of the mountain was not a rock precipice. It was a slope, and dirt, not rock, so it had not stored up the heat of the sun. On the contrary, it was cooled to below freezing by the air descending from the icy crown.

The single jet of hot air rising from the only active crater that had lifted the balloon for a few moments was nothing compared with the chill produced by the twenty square miles of arctic ice crowning the head of Kilimanjaro.

Now the cold down-draught had brought them to eleven thousand on the altimeter. But that was still two miles high.

Roger's teeth chattered with cold. 'We can't go down

too fast for me,' he said, between chatters.

The remark made Hal wake up to a new danger. 'We could go down too fast,' he said.

'The faster the better,' Roger objected.

'No. Trouble with a balloon is, when it's going it tends to keep going. It's hard to stop it. You noticed when we threw out sandbags it was very slow to rise. Same way when it's falling – it doesn't change its mind quickly no matter what you do. It's quite liable to crash into the ground with such a jolt that we'll both be killed. Let's chuck out some more sand.'

Out went more of the precious sandbags. It was no use. The wind rushing down the mountainside carried the balloon swiftly towards complete disaster.

'The trail rope,' Roger exclaimed. 'Wouldn't that slow us down?'

'Why didn't I think of that?' Hal said.

He threw out the trail rope. It was a little more than a hundred feet long. One end of it was fastened to the basket – the other end trailed through the bushes and rocks of the slope.

That was why it was called a trail rope. Its drag over rough ground helped to slow the dangerous rush of the balloon.

At least, that was the idea. But this time the down-coming wind was so strong that the delaying action of the trail rope was slight. They were still going down the slope at the speed of a runaway locomotive.

Would they crash into trees below? Or be ground up on rocks? Hal directed his electric torch downwards. At first it showed him nothing but more slope.

Then he could see the bottom of the slope where the

ground levelled off. 'Fine!' he said. 'Nice soft grass. We won't have too bad a landing after all.'

Roger's sharp eyes saw that the 'nice soft grass' was anything but. As they came closer he could see a thousand daggers waiting to receive them. It was as if the plain was covered with soldiers, each holding his sword erect, and two boys were about to be punctured by the sharp points.

Every leaf stood stiff and straight, about man-high, a good six feet. These sword-like leaves, so pleasantly green that at a distance the whole field had looked like a green meadow, ended in a murderous black needle four or five inches long.

'Sandbags!' Hal yelled. Out they went, but the momentum of the falling balloon still carried it straight down to the field of swords.

'Up into the rigging!' commanded Hal. Like monkeys, or sailors, they went hand over hand up the ropes that suspended the basket.

There was a ripping and tearing sound as the long swords pierced the bottom of the basket and rose so high that the boys had to pull up their legs to avoid the great black needles.

Did they dare come down? Or must they stay up here until morning when the owner of the plantation might possibly come by and rescue them?

The basket was stuck as a man might be stuck fast if he sat down on a porcupine.

'Why does anybody raise such stuff?' Roger demanded angrily. 'What is it anyhow?'

'Sisal,' Hal said.

'And what's sisal?'

'Just the chief export of this country. Looks like cactus. It's a cousin of the century plant.'

'Century plant. That's the one that blooms at the end of a century and then dies.'

'People used to think so. It really doesn't last that long. Only about ten years, then it sends up a tall flower-stalk and blooms and promptly gives up the ghost. Sisal does the same thing.'

He swept the field with his torch. From some of the plants tall spires rose, just one to a plant, up to a height of about twenty feet where the slender stalk was crowned by a great white flower.

'What's it good for, this sisal?'

'Those leaves contain fibres as stiff as wires. The leaves are cut off and taken to a mill where they scrape away the pulp and leave just the fibres. Then they take the fibres and twist them together to make twine and cord and rope and even great cables strong enough to hold an ocean liner.'

'We're in a pretty mess now,' Roger said. 'How do we get loose from those spikes?'

'Let's rock the boat. Both together, from side to side, and we may pull her loose.'

They rocked until they were dizzy. The basket did not budge one inch.

'I think I know what's the trouble,' Hal said. 'Every-one of those leaves has prickles all along the edge, barbed like fish-hooks. We can't move until we get rid of those fish-hooks. I'll see what I can do.'

He eased himself down among the swords. 'Ouch!' he exploded, as the black needles found tender parts of his anatomy. They seemed as sharp as razors. If he escaped the points he scraped his hands on the fish-hooks. He drew his bush-knife and began slashing off the barbs that edged each leaf right down to the floor of the basket.

There was not room for two to work in the basket already populated by several dozen of the enemy, so Roger stayed on watch above. Presently he cried, 'Something funny is happening. The balloon – look!'

Hal stood up and was startled to see that the balloon was leaning far over, away from the mountain. That brought it nearer the ground and if it came a little lower the swords would puncture its skin, the gas would all escape, and the disaster would be complete.

The troublemaker was the wind. It had been coming down the mountainside. Now that the level ground was reached the wind, of course, stopped going down and continued its way west, dragging the great bag with it so that it lay almost on its side nearly within reach of the swords.

Hal worked feverishly. It would be better if he could cut straight through the swords at floor level. He tried it but found it impossible – the 'wires' in the leaf resisted his blade and he did not have room to swing his knife.

He went back to fish-hooks. As he trimmed them off a gummy, soapy juice oozed from the cut places and got on his hands. Now if he had some water he could wash his hands. Africans near the sisal plantations used this ancient soap. Though ancient, it was really more modern than soap – it was nature's own detergent.

Without water, it was just a sticky mess and he got pretty well plastered by it before his trimming job was completed.

'That ought to do it,' he shouted to the monkey in the rigging. 'How's the bag doing?'

'Pulling hard,' Roger said. 'If there was just some way we could ease up on the weight for a minute she might pull free.'

Hal thought fast. He weighed a good one hundred and ninety pounds. If he could just weigh nothing for a second, the balloon would lift.

'I'm getting out,' he said.

'Are you crazy?'

Hal was already clambering out of the basket. He was immediately stabbed in several places by the porcupine quills of the sisal, but he managed to wriggle down among the savage swords and scraping fish-hooks and got his feet on solid ground.

He still held on to the edge of the basket but put no weight on it.

At once he noticed a change. The hydrogen was now able to tear the basket free from the clutch of the sisal. Hal, still hanging on, ran alongside as the basket was dragged over the tops of the plants. The bag rose to a vertical position and the magic carpet began to leave the ground. Hal pulled himself up, and in. His weight caused a momentary sag, then as the last grasping finger-nails of sisal lost their grip the *Jules Verne* rose, free and happy.

'Hal, are you there?' Roger shouted anxiously.

'I'm aboard,' Hal said.

Roger was about to leap down into the basket. 'Don't jump,' Hal warned. 'You might go right through. The floor has been pretty badly riddled by those spines.'

Roger slid gently down into the basket. The torn

weave beneath his feet felt as if it might let him through
at any moment and drop him on the sisal swords.

'A little more of that and we wouldn't have had any
basket,' he said, as they pulled in the trail line. 'What's
the chance of finding a better landing field?'

'Mighty poor. These sisal plantations extend for many
miles. Then the country changes – for the worse.'

Dawn was beginning to colour the sky. Kilimanjaro
was silhouetted like a giant against the morning light.
Ahead, beyond the sisal fields, rose another high hurdle,
Mount Meru, fifteen thousand feet.

'Not again!' exclaimed Roger with sinking heart. 'I've
had enough mountain-hopping. Is this what you meant by
worse ahead?'

'No. I don't think we'll have to top this one. The wind
is going to carry us past it. It's after that that the real fun
begins.'

They slid by Meru with only a few hundred feet to
spare. On the left some miles away lay the town of
Arusha. Hal got it in his binoculars. He hoped someone
might see the fugitive balloon and report its position.
But, so early in the morning, there was not a sign of life
in the streets.

Hal was disappointed, for he knew there would not be
another town for hundreds of miles.

Now the country became worse, as Hal had promised.
It was beautiful, but it offered no landing space for a
balloon swept along by a strong wind. Abrupt hills and
sudden valleys and forests of great trees left only an
occasional small level patch where it would be certain
death to come down, because before the racing balloon

could be stopped it would crash into the trees or rocks on the far side of the clearing.

The only safe place was in the sky – and even there they were not too safe with a torn basket and a gusty wind so powerful that it might tear the bag away from the basket at any moment.

15

The Great Rift

SUDDENLY what looked like America's Grand Canyon opened out beneath. It was about as wide, but not so deep.

'The Great Rift,' Hal said. 'Believed to be the longest canyon in the world. It stretches all the way from the Zambesi River up through Central Africa and North Africa, on up the Red Sea and ends at the Dead Sea – a total length equal to one quarter of the earth's circumference.'

'What made it?'

'Volcanic fires beneath. Most of Africa's volcanoes rise from its sides. Earthquakes keep shaking it. It has a devilish way of shaking cities to bits or sending them up in flames. You remember the Bible story of Sodom and Gomorrah – two cities at the south end of the Dead Sea that were destroyed by earthquake and fire, and people who escaped were told not to look back or they would be turned into pillars of salt. That story may be based on the fact that there really are pillars of salt in that region – and the whole gorge is pretty salty. Of course the Dead Sea is so salty you can't sink in it. And there's a row of salt lakes all along the bottom of the canyon through this part of Africa. There's one ahead right now – Lake Manyara.'

It filled the canyon from cliff to cliff and was so long that the end of it was out of sight. But it wasn't white like salt – it was as pink as a sunset.

'Whoever heard of pink salt?' Roger said, doubting for a moment that his brother knew what he was talking about.

Then something happened that was so weird he could not believe it though he saw it with his own eyes. The whole pink top of the lake rose into the sky and the balloon passed under it.

'What is it – a mirage? I've never seen anything like that in my life.'

'It's not a mirage,' Hal said. 'It's real. Pink flamingoes. Millions upon millions of them live on this lake. When they're alarmed, as they are now by this balloon, they all sail up into the sky in a pink cloud. Except those that can't fly.'

'Why can't they all fly?'

'The soda in the lake hardens on their legs. The big birds can fly in spite of that, but the young ones aren't strong enough. Many of them get so loaded down with the stuff that they can't even swim or walk, much less fly, and they die by the thousands. Game wardens who hate to see beautiful animals die bring in boys and girls from the schools and these young Africans wade into the shallows and break up the big white balls with hammers, taking care of course not to break the leg inside. In that way great numbers of the little birds are saved, but still thousands must die for there just aren't enough kids available to do the whole job.'

'Look at the pink elephants!' exclaimed Roger. 'I thought you had to be drunk to see a pink elephant. And all those other animals near the lake – they're all pink. Or have I got the pink eye?'

It was an amazing sight. The zebras were pink, the giraffes were pink, the rhinos, buffaloes, wildebeest, waterbucks, hippos, hyenas, all pink. Six pink lions emerged from the woods to look up at the balloon. It was a pink world.

Roger looked with astonishment at his pink brother. Hal laughed, and pointed upwards. The sun shone through and between thousands upon thousands of pink wings. The result was that the sun itself could scarcely be seen, but only the glowing pink cloud and a landscape beneath so rosy that you might think you were wearing pink glasses.

The balloon had now left the lake and was travelling over the valley floor. This was the famous Manyara game reserve, protected by towering cliffs, full of tropical vegetation, a paradise for wildlife.

The scene changed suddenly. Now that the balloon had passed, the cloud of flamingoes settled down once more to the lake and the rocks that had been so warm and pink turned cold and grey. A blast of thunder came from the eastern sky. The boys looked back. A thundercloud as black as night was climbing above the horizon. White daggers of lightning stabbed through it.

As if to answer the thunder, the Great Rift talked back with an earth-shaking roar, and landslides of great rocks dislodged from the cliffs by an earthquake crashed down into the valley.

At the same time the god of the winds puffed out his cheeks and turned what had been a steady though strong wind into a violent, gusty gale that tossed the basket into the air and let it down with such a jolt as to break two of the eight lines attaching the basket to the ring.

'Look what's coming,' Roger exclaimed. The western wall of the canyon was rushing towards them. Or so it seemed until you looked down and saw the woodland tearing by underneath.

Roger picked up the trail rope, intending to throw it out and let it drag on the ground to slow down the mad rush of the *Jules Verne*.

'Don't,' Hal warned. 'We can't go low enough to trail a rope. We've got to rise and go over that.'

He nodded at the cliff ahead. The western wall of the canyon rose black and menacing before them. 'We ought to climb to three thousand feet. Don't know whether we can do it or not. Let's chuck out some sand.'

They began to throw out the bags. The supply of sand was getting dangerously low. Hal worried – but Roger hoped that the same thing that had happened at Kilimanjaro would happen again here. An up-current would carry them over the top. 'We'll get into the elevator pretty soon,' he hoped.

Hal was doubtful. 'This isn't that kind of a wind – strong and steady. It's all snorts and sneezes. Hate to worry you, but I'm afraid we have a real cyclone building up. Cyclones have no respect for honest balloonists.'

Roger displayed his knowledge of cyclones. 'A cyclone has a steady wind. It goes round and round in a big circle.'

'Which way?' said Hal.

'Clockwise south of the equator. Anti-clockwise north of the equator.'

'And where are we now?'

'Gee, I hadn't thought of that. We're *on* the equator.'

'So,' Hal said, 'the wind doesn't know which way to go. It just goes mad. It blasts off in all directions. That's why cyclones are so much worse in the tropics than anywhere else. Keep throwing out sand.'

'All of it?'

'Every last bag. It's our only chance.'

Out it all went. Hal hated to see it go, for it meant that from now on they had no means of raising the balloon. They could bring it down by letting out gas. But they could not make it go up. It was at the mercy of wind and sun. Wind might toss it up, sun heating the bag and expanding the hydrogen might carry it up, but any human power to lift it was gone.

They had no time to dwell on these unhappy thoughts, for suddenly a sneeze of the wind god turned the basket completely upside down and the two balloonauts would have fallen to their death if they had not clung to the rim of the basket. As it was, they dangled dangerously over the savage rocks at the foot of the cliff, a thousand feet below.

A wrench of wind reversed the basket and they climbed back in. Their faces were pale with shock. Neither said a word. There were no words strong enough.

The sandbags had done their best and the balloon was rising. But the chance of clearing the top was very slim. There was a moment of hope when the wind turned to bite itself and carried them away from the cliff instead of towards it. The hope died when a whipping blast hurled the basket into the cliff with a crunching, crippling sound that made them fear there would be nothing of their magic carpet left.

For a few breathless moments they stuck there as if plastered to the precipice.

'We could let out some hydrogen and go down,' Roger suggested.

'And be ground up on those rocks? Besides, we have to think of the balloon. It doesn't belong to us. If there's a chance to save it, we've got to do it.'

The wind that had glued the *Jules Verne* to the cliff like a fly to flypaper now had a new and more devilish idea. It gusted in from the side and sent the balloon rolling like a ball along the face of the precipice.

The basket whirled round and round, crashing at every turn into daggers of rock projecting from the cliff. The basket was being mashed into a mush of broken and tangled strands. The points of rock reached out to stab the passengers who hopped continually from one side of the basket to the other in an effort to avoid them. Two more of the ropes suspending the basket were sawed through by rocky knives. Now only four ropes held the basket to the ring above and the extra strain on them might snap them at any moment.

Hal seized some extra rope and tried to repair the broken lines, but the whirling, bumping and bruising made the work almost impossible.

'We're in luck,' Hal gasped.

'What's lucky about this?'

Hal looked up at the bag rolling along the jagged cliff. 'Wonderful that it hasn't been ripped open. That really would finish us off.'

Roger, dizzy and sick from the whirling and bumping,

tried to be grateful. He looked down a thousand feet to the rocks. Yes, it was better to be here than there.

The whirling stopped. A back eddy of wind carried the balloon fifty feet out from the cliff. Then it was thrown in again at such speed that collision with the cliff would surely break the bag or the remaining basket ropes.

It did not quite reach the cliff. A sudden up-blast carried it aloft, up and over the edge of the precipice, out of the diabolical Great Rift, and away at breakneck speed towards the west.

16

Cyclone

THE black cloud had spread to swallow the whole sky. How different from the rosy world of half an hour ago.

Lightning no longer flashed on the eastern horizon. It forked down from the churning clouds directly overhead. Every flash was followed in a split second by a deafening roar.

'Too close for comfort,' Hal said.

Roger guessed his meaning. 'The gas.'

'Right. Hydrogen isn't merely inflammable – it's explosive. Just let one little jag of lightning burn a hole in that bag and there'd be nothing left of either the balloon or us.'

'It wouldn't really act as fast as all that, would it?'

'Well, make a guess,' suggested Hal. 'What do you suppose is the temperature of burning hydrogen?'

'How do I know? Perhaps boiling point; two hundred and twelve, Fahrenheit.'

'Multiply that by twenty-five and you've got it. Hydrogen burns at more than five thousand degrees. One of the hottest flames known. You've seen men welding steel with a blowpipe or blowtorch. Chances are the gas was hydrogen. As soon as it gets out and combines with the oxygen in the air, it explodes. It makes a flame so hot it can cut metal as easily as a knife cuts cheese.'

'Flash, crash!' said the rolling black over their heads. Instinctively they hunched their shoulders as if to protect themselves from the descending danger.

'If hydrogen is so awful,' Roger said, 'why do they use it in balloons?'

'Because it's the lightest of all elements. It lifts the balloon as nothing else could. Next best is helium – but it's heavier and besides you'd have a lot of trouble finding it in Africa.'

The sky was now so dark that the sudden bursts of light hurt the eyes. Roger couldn't help ducking at every new explosion.

'You know,' he said, 'I can think of better things to do than to take a trip through a thunderstorm tied to a bomb.'

Hal laughed. 'Well, since we can't do anything about it, let's forget it. Help me fix these ropes.'

'We have no more line.'

'Then we'll have to cut some pieces from the trail rope.'

He took up the end of the rope. He examined it with interest. 'I remember how this looked when we first got the balloon. The end was frayed out, unravelled. Now look at it.'

The rope ended sharp and clean, not with any ragged tail.

'Know what that means? That rope didn't just come loose from the log. It was cut with a sharp knife.'

Roger stared at the rope. 'Who could have hated us that much?'

'That's easy,' Hal said. 'I can think of three possibilities. King Ku would plainly like to see us snuffed out, and all other white men at the same time – why, remains a mystery. Dugan wants our job and seems willing to stop at nothing to get it. And Basa – I thought we had made him our friend – but perhaps he's still sore.'

It was an unhappy feeling – three deadly enemies on the ground.

But presently there was a fourth. Rain. Not a gentle little shower, but a torrent as if someone above had opened a fire hydrant. It came down from arctic heights. It was bitterly cold, and all the colder because of the cyclonic wind that whipped the boys' wet bodies.

That was bad enough – but the worst thing about it was that it chilled the gas which, contracting and growing heavier, caused the balloon to lose altitude.

They must stay up to stay alive. If the *Jules Verne* were swept along the ground in the arms of the cyclone at seventy or eighty miles an hour, double the speed of a racehorse, anything it happened to strike would destroy it and its passengers. It was like a ship that must be kept well away from rocky coasts during a storm.

A ship can do that, because it has an engine. The engineless balloon was at the mercy of the raging wind.

They got a good idea of the force of the wind when they passed over an African hut just as the palm-leaf roof was lifted off and carried away as if it had been as light as a feather. They caught a fleeting glimpse of the astonished family looking up at their flying roof and trying to protect themselves against the drenching downpour which immediately put out their fire and would soon chill them to the bone.

A great baobab tree struck by lightning blazed fiercely in spite of the rain. This did not make the flyers feel any

more comfortable, knowing that they were tied to a bag of thirty thousand cubic feet of explosive gas.

They were so low now that they were being whipped by the top branches of trees. New holes were torn in the sides and bottom of the basket. But suddenly the world dropped away from under them.

They were over the great Ngorongoro Crater, nearly three thousand feet deep. The floor of this dead volcano covers a hundred and fifty square miles. Within the circle of its mighty wall, a hundred times as high as the Great Wall of China, the fairly level crater-bottom is the home of thousands of wild animals of every description.

There were lakes and pools where hippos and crocodiles enjoyed themselves, and lions, leopards, elephants, rhinos, giraffes, and buffaloes came to drink.

The animals were revealed only when brilliant flashes of lightning illuminated the scene. In between these explosions of light, the black clouds and thundering rain cut off the view. They would have liked to go lower to see this wonderful pageant, but dared not since they must ride high enough to top the wall at the far side of the crater.

The balloon slid over this rampart with only fifty feet to spare and raced on into the great Serengeti Desert. Here there were not only no towns or villages but not even a hut. Sand dunes like those of the Sahara crawled along, driven by the cyclone.

One good thing – the rain was left behind. The sun blazed forth, blinding hot. A terrific sandstorm was in progress. It reached up to scratch the faces of the balloonmen. It blew sand into their eyes and ears, and mouths too if they dared open them.

A gleam of white appeared below. 'What's that?' said Roger.

'A monument to Michael. He died here.'

'Who was Michael?'

'Michael Grzimek was a chap about my age who flew a plane over this desert, trying to make a count of the animals in the annual migration. This very balloon was also used on that same job. Michael and his father made thousands of flights in their small plane back and forth across this desert. Then one day when Michael was flying alone something made the plane crash. I'll bet you can't guess what.'

'A storm like this one?'

'No, it was a perfectly clear, quiet day.'

'Engine trouble?'

'No.'

'His plane collided with another?'

'You're closer to it. There was a collision, but not with another plane. It's hard to believe that a bird could bring down a plane, but that's what happened. A griffin-vulture collided with the right wing and bent it. That blocked the rudder cables and the plane dived and crashed. Michael's body was dragged from under the wreckage. They buried him here and put up that monument. I remember what it says on the monument:

MICHAEL GRZIMEK
He gave all he possessed for the wild
animals of Africa, including his life.

Roger wondered if anybody would say something as nice on the monument to him and his brother. They also had done much for African wildlife. But he decided he'd rather stay alive than have something pretty said about him after he was dead.

They finished repairing the basket ropes. The basket itself they could not repair. They simply avoided the holes that were big enough to fall through, and put as much of their weight as possible on the rim of the basket rather than on the weakened strands under their feet.

'Know something?' Roger said. 'I'm hungry!'

Hal looked up at the desert sun which poured down a merciless torrent of heat. 'And I'm thirsty,' he said.

'Why didn't we think to have a supply of food and water on this thing?'

'Because we never expected to make a trip in it. So long as it was moored in the camp we could easily get to the tent whenever we wanted to eat or drink.'

'If we'd only had time to get our guns out of the car. Then, if we could land, we could shoot a gazelle or something and if we couldn't cook it we could eat it raw and drink its blood.'

'A lot of ifs,' Hal remarked. 'I think your brain is going iffy.'

But he had to admit to himself that his own mind was getting jumpy under the strain of the last dozen hours.

He saw things that weren't there. On the horizon was a village and the villagers had seen the balloon and were coming to help. He knew it wasn't true. There was no village, and no help. But there to the west was certainly a great sheet of water. It must be Lake Victoria. If they should drop into it they would have all the fresh water they could drink.

The peculiar thing about it was that it floated high above the desert. It was a mirage, and he knew it. Lake Victoria did lie in that direction, but more than a hundred miles away.

17

The whirling tower

'I SEE a tower,' Roger exclaimed. 'Straight ahead. We're going to strike it.'

So the poor kid was seeing things too – things that weren't there. 'It's real,' Roger insisted.

Hal rubbed the sand out of his eyes and looked. He saw it too. It was like a pillar in a cathedral, rising straight from the floor so high that the upper end of it was lost in space. Then he recognized it for what it was.

'A twister,' he said. 'Remember?– we've seen them on the ocean. Only there they call it a waterspout. A climbing whirlwind that takes up water with it. Here in the desert it takes up sand. And it will take us up too if we get into it.'

'A tornado?' asked Roger.

'I suppose that's the name for it, except that a tornado usually covers more ground and is a bit less violent. You might call this a tight tornado. It goes up straight and fast like a bullet from a rifle instead of spreading like shot from a shotgun.'

The scream of the whirlwind grew louder as they approached it. The white pillar was moving along the desert floor and there was a chance they might miss it. Oh for an engine or a rudder or some way of changing the course of this crazy balloon!

The moving minaret gave them hope for a moment as it swung out of their path, but then a violent blast from the cyclone drove it back and in the next instant the *Jules Verne* was climbing towards the stars. It whirled sickeningly as it climbed. The needle of the altimeter slid around to its limit but still the balloon went up. The desert below could not be seen now through the sand that filled the air.

'The higher we go the worse it will be coming down,' Hal said.

The ascent seemed slower now. And not so vertical. The pillar was leaning like the Tower of Pisa. The heat of the desert that had started the air on its spiral climb had died out in the cold upper reaches and presently the balloon fell out of the weakened column and began to fall.

'Hang on,' Hal shouted. 'We're in for a hard bump.'

He knew this was stating it very mildly. The bump would not only be hard but perhaps fatal. He had no sand to throw out to delay the downward rush. The gas, chilled by the upper air, had lost much of its lifting power. The up-current of the twister was replaced by a strong down-current, on the principal that whatever goes up must come down.

Since the basket would strike first they must get out of the basket. 'Up into the rigging!' Hal commanded. They clambered up the ropes to the ring.

Now they could see the desert floor rushing up to meet them. Wasn't there anything that could be done?

Hal tried to remember something the warden had told him about just such a situation as this. It was a desperate measure. Hal resolved to try it.

'I'm going to pull the rip line – let out all the gas.'

'Are you off your head?' screamed Roger.

'Probably. But here goes.'

He pulled down with all his strength on the rip line. There was a tearing sound above as a large triangle of fabric was ripped from the top of the bag. Immediately there was a rush of escaping gas and the bag collapsed.

Now, if the plan worked, the twelve lines that ran up from the ring to the balloon would pull the empty bag into something like the form of a parachute and that should ease the fall.

It worked – partly. The drop was slowed, but not enough. They were still sure to strike with terrible force. Directly below was not soft sand but *hamada*, stony desert.

Hal swung himself over beneath his brother. Roger at least would have something soft to land on.

Then came the crash. The basket already full of holes offered no protection against the sharp stones which jabbed their way through it and into Hal's flesh. He struck all the harder because of the weight of Roger's body upon his own. He blacked out.

The billowing folds of the bag settled down upon them as if to give them decent burial.

Roger also was stunned. His brother's body had cushioned his fall and perhaps saved his life, but, after all, Hal's bones had not proved a perfect landing pad.

Slowly he returned to consciousness. At first he hazily thought he was in bed, buried under heavy blankets. Strangely enough, the blankets were whipping up and down, beating the breath out of him. Or perhaps the tent had collapsed and was thrashing about in that screaming wind.

The bed was comfortable beneath him except for a hard bump in the middle. It took him some time to realize that this was his brother's bony hip. And they were not safe in camp, but stranded in the vast wilderness of the Serengeti.

The body beneath him did not move.

'Hal,' he said. No answer. He rolled aside and put his fingers on his brother's wrist. If there was any pulse, it was too faint to feel. He put his ear to Hal's chest. There was no sound, or if there was he couldn't hear it over the shriek of the wind. He put his cheek to his brother's open mouth, hoping to feel the warmth of the breath. But the cyclonic gusts under the billowing bag made that impossible.

Trembling with anxiety, he began to drag the heavy body out from under the balloon. He found himself weak from lack of food and the shock of the fall. At last he got his burden out into the world of sun and sandstorm.

The *Jules Verne* decided it had been earthbound long enough. It rose on a whoop of wind and blew away to the west, it's great empty folds making it look like an enormous flapping bird.

The brisk wind slowly brought Hal back into the land of the living. He opened his eyes. Roger's heart leaped. 'Attaboy!' he said. 'I was afraid you had pooped out.'

Hal looked around dully as if trying to remember where he was and why. Then he looked back at Roger.

'You all right, kid?'

'Just fine.'

'Where's the balloon?'

'Gone with the wind. How about you? I must have landed on you pretty hard.'

'Oh, I'm all right. Think I'll just lie here for a bit. It's so restful on these rocks.'

'You got some nasty gouges. Wish I had some water to wash them out.'

'Don't worry. No germs on those stones. The sun takes care of that.'

Roger looked around at the vacant horizon. 'Wonder how far we'll have to walk.'

'Plenty far,' Hal said, 'and I suppose we'd better get started.'

He struggled to his feet, then went down again with a groan. He put his hand to his right leg.

'Broken?' asked Roger.

'I don't know. Can't tell without a picture. You don't happen to have an X-ray handy?'

'Sorry.'

'I'll try again in a minute.'

When he made another attempt to stand up, he fell on his face. 'It's no good,' he said. 'It won't hold me up. Limp as a piece of spaghetti.'

'Okay,' Roger said. 'Can you take care of yourself while I go for help?'

'Go where? Do you realize what hunters call this part of the Serengeti? Middle of Nowhere.'

Roger stood up and looked around, screwing up his eyes against sand and sun.

'But there must be an African village.'

'Not out here. Too far from water.'

'But see all those animals. Where there are animals there must be water.'

'That sounds logical, but it isn't. Most of the animals you see don't live here. They just pass through, thousands of them, migrating to rivers hundreds of miles north at one time of the year and south at another. And animals that need water frequently don't come here at all.'

'Look here,' said Roger impatiently. 'I can't stand here gabbing. I don't know where I'm going but I'm going.'

'Wait a minute,' Hal said. 'How do you think you will find your way back?'

It was a new and sobering thought. They had no compass, no sextant, no way of fixing their position.

'I have my watch,' Roger said. 'Point the hour hand at the sun – halfway between the hour hand and twelve is south. So I can keep my direction and come back in the opposite direction and I'll find you.'

'Good try,' Hal said, 'but it's not exact enough. You could miss me by thirty miles.'

'I have another idea,' Roger said. 'I'll drag a stick – then follow the line back.'

'What kind of a mark do you think your stick would make on this rocky ground? And when you come to stand, the mark you make would be covered by drifting sand in half an hour. I think you'd better just go ahead and forget about me. No use of both of us staying to feed the vultures.'

'Don't talk nonsense,' Roger said sharply. His eyes swept over the plain. A quarter of a mile away a herd of zebras was going north. They kept in close formation. Following them were several hundred wildebeest. They too kept close together, not scattered all over the desert.

'I'm going over there to take a look,' Roger said.

The animals refused to change their course even when he came close.

Just as birds fly south to spend the winter in the tropics, and fly north at the beginning of summer, so the warmth-loving animals of Africa follow the sun.

This was one of many animal trails across the Serengeti. Thousands upon thousands of feet had ground a trail through stones or sand a yard deep and several hundred yards wide.

Roger went back to his brother. 'The beasties have solved our problem. They've made a perfectly grand road – all I have to do is to follow it until I find somebody. Then I'll bring him back by the same trail.'

'Don't forget that it isn't really a road,' Hal said. 'I mean it doesn't lead to any village or camp. In fact the migrating animals try to stay away from any spot occupied by humans. You might go a hundred miles without finding anything on two legs, except an ostrich.'

'Well, can you suggest anything better?'

'No, I can't. Go ahead, and good luck.'

Roger whipped off his bush-jacket. 'You'd better have this. It will get cold tonight.'

'You'll need it yourself.'

'No I won't. I'll be walking. That'll keep me plenty warm.'

18

Night walk

IGNORING his brother's protests, Roger set out into the unknown.

It was really a pleasure to be walking once more, after being cooped up so long in the flying basket. He left the animal-made road to the animals and strode along beside it. If he made good time, perhaps he might even find somebody before dark.

He kept straining his eyes for the smoke of a camp-fire or cabin. There was no sign that any man lived here or had ever lived here. Yet he did not feel alone – so long as the sun shone and so long as he had the animals for company.

He admired the sleek striped coats of the zebras and laughed at the long homely faces of the wildebeest and marvelled to see the giraffes cover ten feet at each step.

Roger was fast on his feet, yet he was surprised at how easily these travellers passed him. Here came a herd of elephants. These huge beasts could be expected to move slowly – yet they went by as if he had been standing still. As for the gazelles, they could not even wait for the elephants, but leaped through between them and sped on towards grass and water who knows how many miles away. Perhaps they knew.

The equatorial sun blazed down fiercely and the sweat

streaming down his forehead together with the flying sand made mud in his eyes. He wished he could cover them, but he had to see. But he didn't have to breathe sand – he got out his handkerchief and tied it over his nose and mouth. Now he understood why the Tuaregs of the Sahara wear veils.

Hunger gnawed at his insides. It was almost twenty-four hours since he had had a bite to eat. But he told himself that he was not suffering any more than his animal companions. An elephant, for example, needs six hundred pounds of grass and leaves a day to keep that huge machine in operation. That was why these beasts did not stop to spread their ears when they saw him, or threaten him with raised trunks. They were only in-terested in getting on as fast as possible towards the dinner table. Their babies had to run to keep up with them, and tried to snatch a little milk from their mothers while going at full speed.

Roger, burning with thirst, envied the baby elephants. They didn't know how lucky they were to get even those few driblets of moisture.

Roger imagined himself in a lush meadow beside a stream. He dropped down on his stomach and buried his face in the water and gulped great draughts of the sweetest liquid on God's earth. Then he lay in the grass and slept.

But his legs were still moving and the sand was cut-ting into his eyes. And his injured brother was depend-ing upon him to go and come again with help.

The sunset was not a thing of beauty. It was not red nor pink nor golden. Seen through flying sand, the sun was a bilious yellow ball and the whole western sky

looked as if it had jaundice. The dark closed down swiftly. And a boy who had thought he was a man discovered that after all he was only thirteen years old and very much alone in spite of the animal train that moved beside him.

In fact the animals seemed to change their character. Instead of being pleasant companions they were now perils of the night. At this hour the carnivores were likely to attack anything that couldn't defend itself, and of all creatures man was the most defenceless.

In the daytime, Roger had thought of the animals as friends. In the dark, the desert seemed full of enemies. What beasts did he have most reason to fear? He began to list them in his mind.

First, the lion. This was lion country. There were said to be more lions in the Serengeti than in any other equal area in all Africa – in fact, more than anywhere else in the world. There were known to be man-eaters among them. Lions wounded by hunters develop very bad tempers and would attack any man, women, or child they happened to find. Night was the time when they were most active.

Second, the leopard. He was even more of a night-lover than the lion. He was seldom seen by day. Now he was most certainly on the prowl. Roger began to see spots in every direction.

Third, the caracal. It was a desert cat, quite at home in the Serengeti. Though smaller than a lion or leopard, it was even more savage and did not hesitate to attack anything ten times its size.

Fourth, the hyena. He had already seen hyenas in the procession. With the coming of night, they were quite likely to begin to think about fresh meat, either animal or human.

Fifth, the wolf-like jackal. Also its cousin, the Abyssinian wolf. One jackal was not to be feared. But multiply one jackal's courage by twelve or twenty, and the pack was quite capable of making trouble.

Sixth the snake. Such snakes as the cobra, the mamba, and the python would not travel by day because they could not stand the heat of the sun. They would lie under a bush or in a hole until night came, then they would be on their way. Besides these travellers, Roger knew that there were other snakes that lived permanently in the desert, and liked it. The horned viper and the sand viper buried themselves in the sand and were too sluggish to get out of your way – but if you stepped on one he would strike like lightning. By daylight, you might see a part of the snake through the sand and avoid it. But now in the dark, every step Roger took was taken with tingling muscles ready to leap if anything squirmed underfoot.

Of course even the grass-eating animals were more dangerous at night than in the daytime. The rhinos were more irritable because they could not see well, the buffaloes would horn anything they did not understand, a bull elephant straying from the track might easily bring down his huge foot with ten tons behind it upon a boy and reduce him to a pancake.

But, in spite of all his wild imaginings, there was one enemy he had not thought of. He did not think of it even when he stepped on something that seemed to be a rock and it rolled under his feet. He began to fall but did not reach the ground before he was struck a terrific blow and knocked straight into a pair of huge jaws.

But as the teeth closed on his arm, he knew. It was a crocodile; but who would have thought this water-loving beast would come trundling over the desert? Still, he remembered the statement by Colonel Stevenson-Hamilton, once warden of Kruger National Park: 'By night these reptiles often travel great distances overland.' If

their water-hole goes dry, there is nothing they can do but seek another.

Here was one croc who was quite willing to give up seeking long enough to grab an unexpected but very juicy dinner. His powerful tail had thrashed Roger within reach of his jaws. Roger did his best to pull loose. He was held as if in a vice. The croc's teeth turn inward like those of a python, so once it has taken hold it is not easily persuaded to let go.

The beast was quite satisfied to hang on, and wait. His teeth were adapted for holding, not biting or chewing. He would just patiently wait for his victim to die, and then wait some more for the body to rot, and when it was sufficiently tender he would break it up with his sledgehammer tail and swallow it, chunk by chunk.

A brilliant prospect, Roger thought. To die quickly was not so bad, but to die by inches and by hours of pain and starvation, that was something else. And there was his brother's life to think of as well as his own.

One thing that made Roger unwilling to spend hours or days in the croc's company was the creature's breath. This beast had a bad case of halitosis. The birds that go into a croc's open mouth as he lies asleep on the sand and pick the rotten meat out from between his teeth had in this case not done a good job. Altogether, Roger found his new companion most unpleasant.

What could he do? He had heard that you could free yourself from a croc by punching your thumbs into his eyes. Since Roger's left arm was in the creature's jaws, he could use only his right hand. He dug his thumb deep into the croc's left eye and felt it squash under the pressure. The great jaws did not open.

Roger dug his thumb into the other eye. He hated to do it. He could sympathize even with a stinking croc. The clutch on his arm let up for just an instant. It was long enough for Roger to jerk his arm free. Then the great rows of teeth clacked shut again with a noise like that of a steel trap. The powerful tail swung around to catch the victim before he had a chance to escape. But in that fraction of a second Roger had rolled like a ball out of reach of both tail and teeth. Then he leaped to his feet and ran, for he knew that the crocodile, which seems such a sleepy and slow-moving monster, can move incredibly fast when it wants to.

When he was sure that he had out-distanced his enemy, he slowed to a walk, but he was remarkably careful from now on not to step on another rock that was not a rock.

19

Saved by lions

HAL shivered. He was grateful for Roger's bush-jacket, but even with it to cover him his inactive body was chilled.

Someone wrote a song once containing the words, 'Till the sands of the desert grow cold'. The writer evidently supposed that the desert never grows cold.

He should visit the Serengeti or the Sahara any night of the year, even in midsummer. Very shortly after the sun goes down the desert floor loses its heat. The night winds sweeping down from the snows of Kilimanjaro and Mount Kenya and the Mountains of the Moon – or, in the case of the Sahara, from the snow-capped Atlas – carrying off the remaining warmth of the desert. This chill wind blows so strongly that it may even pick up the tent in which you are sleeping and carry it off, leaving you quite exposed to the icy gale.

This night it was colder than usual because of the cyclone. It was dying, but still strong enough to whip Hal with sand and small stones. The sand got up his nose and made breathing difficult. He covered his nose and mouth with the edge of the bush-jacket. If there had been a sand dune handy, he would have burrowed his way into it as the nomads do. There he would stay until the storm passed.

But even this small comfort was denied him. Instead of sand, he had a bed of sharp stones.

His leg hurt badly. He would have given a lot for something to quiet the pain. He would have given even more for a drink of water. Sun and wind and worry had dried out his body and worn his nerves. He tossed about, unable to sleep.

It was just as well that he remained awake or he would not have heard the hyenas. His first warning was a stirring of the stones beside him and a snuffling sound. He uncovered his face to find a hyena's nose within inches of his own. At this movement the animal backed away with a peculiar little laugh.

Hal looked about. He could dimly see a circle of black shapes all around him. A ring of hyenas sitting on their haunches watching him.

He knew that a hyena is generally considered a coward. If a man is on his feet the beast will not touch him. But if a man lies asleep or sick or dying he is fair game for this killer. In such a case, the hyena is even bolder than a lion, particularly if he is not alone but backed up by a good number of his pals. Many a hunter sleeping in the open has lost a foot or a hand or even a life to these sly beasts.

Hal struggled up on to his feet. Or rather foot. He could not bear to put any weight on his right leg. He must stand only on his left.

Standing on one foot may be natural for a stork but a man cannot do it for long. Especially if he's in pain, and weak from lack of food.

The hyenas did not slink away, nor did they come closer. They continued to sit in a circle about ten feet

off. A little ripple of laughter went round the circle –
but the laugh of the 'laughing hyena' is not merry. It is
so evil that it chills the blood.

Hal stuck it out for perhaps a quarter of an hour, then
he slumped to the ground. A low growl went around the
circle. The animals stood up, and one or two of the
bravest, or hungriest, pressed in a little closer.

Hal wished fervently that he had something more
deadly than his knife. However, he drew it from its
sheath and prepared to defend himself. One hyena coming too near received a kick from Hal's good foot and
ran away howling, but he immediately returned.

Hal swung the bush-jacket around his head. Each
animal stepped back to let it pass and then pushed in a
little closer. They were not to be kept from their dinner
by a bush-jacket.

As he felt the hot breath of the animals on his face he
realized it was time to use his knife. He plunged it into
the neck of the nearest animal and the beast laughed as
it died.

Immediately the other hyenas leaped upon their dead
companion and tore him limb from limb and devoured
the flesh before it turned cold. They did not pick the
bones – instead, they crushed them to bits between their
powerful teeth and swallowed them. They licked the
blood from the stones. In five minutes there was nothing
left of the dead hyena, and they turned their attention
once more to Hal.

Another hyena was killed, and eaten. But this did not
satisfy those who had dined. Instead, the taste of blood
had made them more furious so they forgot all caution.
They pressed in from all sides, biting, snapping, laugh-

ing, while Hal kicked with his good foot, swung the bush-jacket with one hand and plied the knife with the other.

One hyena leaped upon his chest and brought his open jaws close to Hal's face. Hal stabbed straight up into the animal's body. The blade stuck in the beast's ribs. The hyena jumped away, locked its jaws on the handle of the knife, jerked it out and flung it on the rocks well beyond Hal's reach.

Hal's strength was going fast. He could no longer kick with force, and waving the bush-jacket did no good. He wrapped the bload-soaked garment around his head to protect his face. He pushed hyenas away with his bare hands. They always came back.

He knew the game was up. It was only a matter of minutes now. Roger would come back to find no sign of his brother. Except perhaps the knife – it was too hard to swallow.

Not only would he be devoured but his bloody cloth-ing as well. Even the blood-stained stones would be swallowed. The hyena habitually swallows stones to aid his digestion. Such hard articles as Hal's wrist-watch and the few coins in his pockets would go down with the stones.

Everything would be left clean and neat. You had to give the hyena credit for that – he didn't leave any mess lying about. He was an even better scavenger than the vulture.

Hal had never been one to call for help. But now he called. A voice would carry a long way across the desert. Perhaps Roger was still within earshot. Or perhaps some African was wandering in the night.

He shouted in English. He shouted in Swahili. He

shouted in no language at all. He listened hard for a response, but he heard nothing – except the distant roar of lions.

At the moment the hyenas were busy finishing off the beast that Hal had just knifed. Hal, drained of all energy, sank into unconsciousness.

He did not know how many seconds, or minutes, he lay thus before he was roused by the growls of lions. These were followed at once by the uproar of a fight between the hyenas and the newcomers. This was very brief, for a hyena has no wish to tangle with his most powerful enemy, the lion. Squealing in pain and yipping with terror, the hyenas made off across the desert.

Hal did not feel he had made a very good bargain. His shouts had attracted animals far more dangerous than the hyenas. But perhaps they had gone away. Cautiously, he looked out from under the jacket. No, they were still close to him, and creeping closer – three bristling bodies silhouetted against the stars. They began to sniff at his body.

Suppose they were man-eaters – there were many such in the Serengeti. Then another thought struck him. Suppose they were not man-eaters. The blood on him was not human blood, but the blood of hyenas, and the lion savagely hates the hyena.

But the lions were making sounds that did not seem very savage. They were gurgles and half-purrs, the sounds of pleasure that might come from a dog or cat. Then one of the visitors lay down on its back close beside him with all four paws in the air and rubbed its soft whiskers against his face. Another patted him gently with its paw as if inviting him to play. These animals

were evidently delighted to find a human. They must have known humans, and loved them. They were attracted by the human voice. They had come when he shouted.

He puzzled over it. What was it he had read in the Nairobi newspapers? Something about the famous Joy Adamson and her three pet lions.

Joy was the wife of a game warden near the border of Sudan. She had rescued a little orphan lioness whom she named Elsa and had lovingly cared for it from babyhood to motherhood. Elsa gave birth to three cubs and Joy cared for them also. Two were males and one a female. She called them Jespah, Gopa, and Little Elsa. Mother Elsa died. The three cubs grew to full size under Joy's care.

Though she didn't want to part with them, Joy felt they should be free to live with other lions. So she brought them to the lion country of the Serengeti and set them free.

One of them, Jespah, had been shot with an arrow by an African hunter. The shaft had broken off, leaving the arrow-head in his flesh. Doctors had advised against an operation to remove the arrow-head because the shock might kill the lion. They believed that in time the thing would fall out of its own accord.

Joy was anxious about the lions after they had been released, particularly about Jespah who was still suffering from his wound. She stayed in the Serengeti, hoping to see her lions again, and give them help if they needed it.

And that brought the story up to date. Hal had read that Joy was now living in the Seronera Safari Camp in the heart of the Serengeti and all day every day she searched the great desert for her lions.

Perhaps these were Joy Adamson's lions – perhaps they weren't. Her animals had been taught to answer to their names. Hal would try an experiment.

'Gopa!' he said distinctly. The lion that had wanted to play came sharply to attention, raising his ears. 'Elsa!' The young lioness that had been wandering about stopped short and looked at Hal. 'Jespah!' The male who had been lying on his back came up promptly on all four feet.

Hal passed his hand along this animal's flank. He came to something metallic projecting from the rump. There was no doubt about it – it was an arrow-head, and these friendly beasts were Joy Adamson's lions.

She didn't want them back – she only wanted to know if they were well. Hal, if he should ever see her, could report that they were.

The three lions lay down beside him. Thus guarded, Hal relaxed and slept.

20

The man in the canyon

ROGER plodded on into the new day.

He hardly knew it was day. His mind was numb. Hunger, thirst, fatigue, loss of sleep, had almost deprived him of his wits. He only knew that he had to keep going.

His bleary eyes kept searching the landscape for some sign of human life. The desert stretched away to the horizon without a hut, without even a tree or bush. The animals in the migration trail seemed as weary as he was. The weaker ones fell down with a despairing cry and the others staggered around them or walked over them.

It was about mid-morning when Roger noticed a break in the plain off to the left. He hobbled over towards it and suddenly found himself on the edge of a precipice looking down into a canyon several hundred feet deep.

He had been almost asleep on his feet – but he came to with a start when he saw at the bottom of the gorge some things that looked very much like tents and some black objects moving about that might be human beings.

New energy pulsed through his tired muscles. He scrambled and slid down the steep slope and approached the tents. A white-haired man in dusty overalls noticed him and came out to meet him.

Roger's brain cleared. He knew who this man was. He had seen his picture in the magazines. He was a famous scientist, Dr Louis Leakey. And this must be Olduvai Gorge where Dr Leakey and his wife had patiently dug for twenty years, and had finally thrilled the world with their discovery of the fossils of men who had lived here two million years ago.

Respectfully, he shook the hand of the great man.

'I know you are Dr Leakey,' he said. 'My name is Roger Hunt.' He said it shyly, for he was sure the name would mean nothing to the doctor.

'Hunt!' exclaimed Leakey. 'Not one of the Hunts who cleared the poachers out of Tsavo?'

Roger nodded, surprised to discover that the Hunts also had their small bit of fame.

'I thought I saw in the papers that you were after man-eaters,' Dr Leakey went on. 'And you were using a balloon as a look-out.'

'Yes,' Roger said. 'But the balloon was cut loose and we drifted here. We had to junk the balloon. My brother is badly hurt.'

'You don't look too well off yourself. We were just going to have lunch. Will you join us? Then we'll go and pick up your brother.'

In a sort of dream, Roger ate, drank, then found himself in a Land-Rover with Dr Leakey himself at the wheel following the migration trail back to the spot where Hal lay.

Hal's friends of the night had left him with the coming of dawn. His leg was swollen and the others had to help him into the Land-Rover. There a canteen of water and some food brought from the Leakey camp revived him.

Dr Leakey looked at the leg.

'Just a bad strain,' he said. 'You'll be all right in a day or two. I'll take you to Seronera Safari Camp. They have a small plane – perhaps you can charter it back to Tsavo.'

For the first few miles they ran alongside the migrating herds.

'It's a strange thing,' said Dr Leakey. 'These animals – they're so much smaller than the ones two million years ago. The rhino then was twice the size of the black rhino today. The baboons, kudus, ostriches, pigs, sheep – they were all giants.'

'Were men giants too?' Hal asked.

'No, curiously enough, they were only about two thirds the size of modern man. During all these years while animals have become smaller, man has been growing.'

'Your Olduvai Gorge has been called the cradle of man,' Hal said. 'Scientists used to think that Asia was the place where man originated.'

'Not any more,' said Leakey. 'Now it is pretty well accepted that Man One must have been African, not Asian.'

He modestly neglected to mention that this change in scientific thinking was due to his own excavations in East Africa.*

The Land-Rover left the animal trail and struck off to the north-east. There was no road. Dr Leakey kept consulting his compass.

* Dr Leakey, who died in 1973, was a very real person. For the story of his remarkable discoveries, see *National Geographic Magazine*, February 1965.

The desert was now neither stones nor sand, but hummocks – little mounds of dirt about a foot high topped with tough grass. The jolting was painful for a fellow with a bad leg and Hal more than once almost lost consciousness before they arrived at Seronera.

Seronera was no town or village, but just a camp of a dozen rondavels – round huts roofed with thatch. It was in the heart of a pleasant oasis watered by a stream, abounding in trees, and completely surrounded by lions.

Hal waited on the airstrip while his brother went to the nearby dispensary and returned with a pair of crutches.

In the small office the newcomers found the warden and a lady who was introduced as Joy Adamson. She was slender and attractive and it was hard to think of her as the playmate of four powerful lions, Elsa and her three big cubs. She could hardly believe her ears when Hal told her he had slept with her lions.

'How do you know they were mine?'

'They answered to their names.'

'Did you find the arrow-head?'

'I did.'

'Was the wound festering?'

'No. Jespah was in good shape, and so were the others.'

He told her how he had been attacked by hyenas – how the lions had scared them off – how they had protected him the rest of the night. 'And for all this,' he added, 'I am very grateful – grateful to you.'

'Why to me?'

'If you hadn't loved those lions and taught them to be friends of man I wouldn't be alive now.'

21

Unhappy man-eater

RETURNING by small plane to Tsavo, the boys told
Tanga what had happened and Tanga had news for
them.

'It's about Dugan,' he said. 'Dugan wanted to show us
what a great lion-killer he was so we would get rid of
you and take him back. He went prowling around, looking for a lion. Yesterday just after the sun went down he
thought he saw one. He couldn't see very plainly because
it was behind some bushes. He fired at it, and it fell. He
went to look at it and found it was no lion – it was a
cow. He dug a hole and pushed it in and covered it up
and hoped nobody would be the wiser.

'This morning the people of Gula village missed a
cow. They followed its tracks out of the village and
down the hill, through the woods and out into the plain.
Where the tracks ended they saw a pile of fresh dirt and
dug up their cow. There was a bullet-hole just back of
the left shoulder.

'They're pretty smart – those Gula fellows. They knew
that you two and Dugan were the only men allowed to
carry guns. You were away, so it must have been Dugan.
About twenty of them came down here to the camp,
dragged him out of his tent, and put him on the first
train to Nairobi. Before he left they made him admit that

he wanted you out of the way, and that he untied your tent flaps in the hope that Black Mane would kill you. If he comes back, they will kill him. So now you are free of Dugan.'

The boys were happy that they were rid of this pesky fellow, yet they were a bit sorry for the cow-killer. And not quite sure about Tanga.

'How do *you* feel about it?' Hal asked. 'Perhaps you wish you'd hired him back. We certainly haven't been too successful.'

Tanga smiled. 'After all,' he said, 'you haven't done too badly. It took Colonel Patterson nine months to get two man-eaters. You already got one – and I still have faith you're going to get the big fellow with the black mane. By the way, I fed your cub while you were gone.'

Flop welcomed them to the tent with wild leaps and lickings and grinding purrs. They fed him and themselves and collapsed on their beds, ready to sleep a night and a day to make up for the hardships aboard the *Jules Verne* and in the Serengeti.

It must have been two or three hours later that they were wakened by a strange sound. It was not loud, but it was close. It was too deep to be the snarl of a hyena. It was not a growl but a sort of moaning, the voice of sadness and loneliness. It went round and round the tent.

Hal turned on his flashlight. Flop was acting strangely. The little cub was tumbling around inside the tent under the beds and under the chairs, following the sound outside. He answered the moaning voice with plaintive little miaows.

'Could it be Black Mane out there?' guessed Roger. 'Could this be his cub?'

The sound outside was farther away now. Then it faded in the distance.

'Perhaps we can catch up with him,' Hal said.

They flung on their clothes, grabbed their revolvers, and crept out. Hal hobbled along quite easily on his crutches. They followed the sound to the trees. They brushed aside the bushes and their flashlight suddenly picked up two great yellow eyes.

A huge, black-maned lion lay on the very spot where they had found and killed the lioness and taken its cub.

It was an easy shot. The boys raised their revolvers. They fully expected the lion to growl savagely and make ready to spring upon them. But he seemed hardly to notice them. He was wrapped up in his own miseries, and kept moaning softly.

It was all too plain. Black Mane was mourning the loss of his mate and his cub. Lions are not like some animals which care little about family life. It is lion nature to take one mate and one alone and be true to her to death and beyond. And unlike some animal fathers, the male lion cares deeply for his cubs.

It was impossible not to feel sorry for Black Mane. The boys felt they were to blame for his unhappiness. They had killed his mate and taken his cub.

And it seemed unsportsmanlike to shoot a lying-down lion. You wouldn't shoot your worst enemy unless he was on his feet and attacking you. Besides, the boys were not trained as killers. From earliest childhood they had been taught to take animals alive. They had been with animals so much that they had come to share their feelings. The great sorrowful eyes of Black Mane looked straight into their hearts.

But they could not forget that he was a man-eater. He was guilty of the death of many men. And the boys had taken on the job of ridding the Tsavo region of man-eaters. It wasn't fair to the men to let this animal go free, and yet how could you murder this magnificent beast in cold blood?

Roger lowered his gun. 'Let's not do it,' he said.

'We've got to,' said his brother.

'No we don't.'

'What else can we do?'

'Take him alive,' proposed Roger.

Hal lowered his gun, glad of anything that would delay the moment of murder.

'I suppose you know what you're saying,' Hal said. 'We don't have our men to help us. How could we take him alive?'

'I don't know,' Roger admitted. 'But there must be some way.'

Still arguing, they found themselves walking back to the tent. They had missed their great opportunity to kill a savage man-eater.

'Why do you suppose he didn't jump us?' asked Roger.

'His mind was occupied with something else – loss of his mate and cub.'

'Poor son of a gun,' Roger said. 'I never would have thought lions could be that sentimental.'

'They're very affectionate animals,' Hal explained.

'Not only with their family, but with other lions too. One day in a pride of fourteen lions I saw a big male go around and rub his head affectionately against every one of the fourteen. You'd never see a leopard doing that – he thinks only of himself. A tiger likes to live alone. But a lion wants other lions around him. And he'll help any one that needs help. The warden at Kitani told me about a young lioness that fed an old one. That doesn't happen often in nature. It's customary for the old to take care of the young, not for the young to take care of the old. This young lioness kept making raids on the chickens back of Mac's Inn at Mtito Andei. The innkeeper saw the old lion eating a chicken and blamed it for the raids and shot it. He shot the wrong animal. The warden discovered that it was the young one who had been stealing the chickens to feed her old friend who was unable to hunt for herself. And it's very common for an old male and a young one to team up together. The old one gives advice and the young one does the actual killing. It's a way of combining the experience of age and the strength of youth.'

'What's an old lion, anyway? How long do they live?'

'About twenty years. But some do much better than that. A lion that was kept as a pet in the Tower of London during the eighteenth century lived seventy years. Of course he was protected. Out in the wilds a lion too old to defend itself is generally destroyed by hyenas.'

A slight sound made Hal swing around and raise his flashlight. 'Black Mane is following us. I still think it's our duty to shoot that beast. We can't take him alive. Don't expect me to be a party to any such crazy scheme.'

'Very well,' said Roger stubbornly. 'I'll do it alone.'

'Alone! I *thought* you were out of your head. Now I'm sure of it.'

They entered the tent. Flop was miaowing for another feeding. Roger put a bowl of the prepared milk on the ground and helped the cub hold the bamboo tube. Hal directed his spotlight upon the operation.

So they did not notice when Black Mane put his head in between the still open flaps and saw what was going on.

For a long minute he stood and looked. Then he growled deeply, pushed his way into the tent, took his cub by the nape of the neck and made off with it towards the woods.

'Well, that's that,' Hal said. 'I hope you're satisfied. Now you've lost both your lion and your cub.'

But Roger refused to be discouraged. He looked at the bowl of milk on the ground. 'I have a hunch they'll be back.'

'Nonsense. Black Mane got what he wanted – his cub. Why should he come back?'

'In two or three hours that cub will start miaowing. He's too young to eat meat. He has to have milk. How do you suppose his father's going to give it to him?'

22

Capture of Black Mane

HAL slept again. Roger lay awake, listening.

The sounds of the African night always fascinated him. He had come to know the calls of many of the animals. This night, all the beasts seemed to be on the prowl.

He could hear the crank-crank of the warthog, the deep ho-ho of the hippo at the nearest water-hole, the gravelly growl of a leopard in the woods, the yip-yip of jackals, the poor imitation of a lion's roar produced by the hyena.

Hal had tied the tent flaps to keep out unwelcome visitors. Roger slipped out of bed and untied them. This was strictly against camp rules.

There is nothing to prevent animals from wandering around your tent in an African camp. No camp is fenced in. A village may be fenced to keep animals out of the gardens. But a camp of hunters or railway workers has no gardens. A safari camp may be used for only one night or at most for a few weeks and so is not worth the trouble of fencing. But you are supposed to keep your tent tightly closed. Then rhinos, elephants, lions, and all other night visitors will probably walk by without giving you a call.

Roger knew very well that it was risky to leave the

tent flaps open. But he had taken his revolver and a flashlight to bed with him and had no intention of going to sleep.

During the first hour he was left in peace. Halfway through the second, he became aware of the sound of heavy breathing. Then something brushed across him. He put out his hand and grasped something round and slithering – it must be a great snake.

He reached for his flashlight and turned it on. The 'great snake' was an elephant's trunk, exploring the inside of the tent in search of food.

Roger played the light straight into the elephant's eyes and the surprised beast backed out with low rumblings of disappointment and annoyance.

In the third hour Roger had to frighten away an inquisitive hyena and an impertinent baboon. He was almost ready to give up when he heard a soft miaow. His flashlight revealed the twisting little body of Flop dangling from the jaws of the monster of the black mane.

Roger directed his spotlight upon the bowl of milk. Black Mane dropped the cub which flopped its way directly to the bowl and tried to drink. Roger reached down and helped it to hold the bamboo tube and the cub sucked greedily. Black Mane stood by, watching warily, ready to snatch up his cub and make off at the first sign of trouble.

'What's going on?' came from the other bed.

'Pipe down,' whispered Roger.

Hal opened sleepy eyes. If what he saw amazed him he made no sign. He took in the situation at a glance and remained quiet.

Black Mane gradually relaxed. Finally he lay down

and began to growl – but it was not exactly a growl. It sounded like a purr coming out of a cave.

Hal had to admit that his young brother had done pretty well. For the moment at least, he had subdued the King of Beasts. But what could he do now? How was he going to take Black Mane alive? This was a test of the boy's manhood. Hal decided he would not interfere in any way – he would let his brother work it out for himself.

'Hold the tube,' Roger whispered. 'I'm going out.'

Hal reached out and took the tube. The cub continued to drink. Roger very cautiously slipped out of bed. Black Mane half rose and this time his purr was a growl. He settled down again as Roger quietly left the tent.

Pale dawn was lighting the sky. The animals that felt free to visit the camp during the night had retreated to the forest. Roger ran to the station. The door to the waiting-room was never locked. He went in and found the place empty.

On the wall was an old-fashioned telephone. It was the only telephone near by – but twenty miles away there was another at the headquarters of the warden, Mark Crosby. Roger waited impatiently until Crosby got on the line.

'This is urgent,' he told Crosby. 'Slap a lion cage on a Power-wagon and rush it up here. The cage has to be plenty large – he's a whopping big lion.'

'Right,' said Crosby. 'Do you want me to send any of your men?'

'That won't be necessary. But hurry – he's apt to walk out on me any minute.'

He ran back to the tent, entered cautiously, and

slipped into bed. Hal looked at him inquiringly.

'Cage coming,' Roger said.

Hal smiled. So far, so good. But how would the youngster get the lion to go into the cage? Had he thought of that?

The cub had finished his breakfast and was pawing the last drops of milk from his soft little whiskers. Roger snapped on the leash that held him to the bed – just in case he might take a notion to wander out and take his father with him.

The big lion was getting restless. He might try to carry away his cub before the car arrived. It was an anxious half hour before the Power-wagon rolled into the camp.

The sound did not disturb Black Mane since lions are not at all worried by cars.

Roger went out. The African driver already had the cage door up and the ramp in place at the tail-gate. Roger re-entered the tent, untied the leash from the bed, and led the waddling little cub out of the tent and up the ramp and into the cage. He went all the way to the back of the cage and tied the leash to one of the bars.

He came out to find Black Mane already coming up the ramp.

The lion paused at the door of the cage. This was something new to him. But he had been in tents, and this didn't look as dangerous as a tent. You couldn't see out when you were in a tent. Here you could see between the bars in all directions.

Besides, his cub was calling for him, Flop was trying to come to him, pulling at his leash. Black Mane joined him and the youngster expressed his pleasure by stand-

ing on his hind legs and biting his father's ears and nose.

Roger loosened the trip-line and the cage door slipped down into place.

Hal had come out of the tent with his rifle, expecting that he might have to use it to save his brother's life. The foolish boy carried no weapon – no rifle, no revolver, not even a knife. He was armed with nothing except the fact that he had fed Black Mane's cub, and Black Mane had seen him do it. Thanks to this understanding between boy and beast, and thanks to the lion's desire to be with his cub, a deadly man-eater had been conquered without the firing of a shot.

Men coming out of the tents could hardly believe what they saw – the monster of the black mane behind bars. It couldn't be true – yet there it was. There was no sign of a fight. Both boys were alive and without a scratch. In the

African mind there was only one answer. It must have been done by magic.

The men broke into cheers. The lion began to look around nervously with a deep growl. Hal motioned the men to be silent, and Roger, standing beside the cage, spoke soothingly to Black Mane and Flop. Then he told the driver to drive – slowly – to Crosby's camp.

He continued to stand beside the cage speaking in quiet tones to his two friends. Animals along the way, seeing the gigantic lion, made off into the forest.

A ranger at Kitani Safari Lodge saw the car coming and ran in to call the warden. Crosby was out and waiting when the Power-wagon with its strange load came to a halt.

'I've brought you a couple of guests,' Roger said.

Crosby stared. In his long experience he had seen some remarkable sights but nothing quite like this.

'How did you do it?'

'I didn't do it,' Roger said. 'The cub did it.' And he told how it had all come about. Then he said, 'Can you take care of these beasties until we can ship them out to some zoo?'

'Of course. Leave them here as long as you like. We'll keep them in the same cage, and they'll have royal treatment, you may be sure.'

'Could you give me a lift back to the station?'

In a Land-Rover Roger returned to the railway camp. He slipped through the crowd of men who flocked out to congratulate him, got into his own tent and relaxed on the bed.

Now that it was all over – the sleepless night, the anxiety, the strain – he felt as if he would come apart.

His nerves were jumping and his face was hot. Hal felt his pulse. It was rattling along like a machine gun.

The men who had decided that Roger was a white witch doctor should see him now. He was no magician, but just a boy who had used his head and was very tired. He needed aspirin and sleep and he got both.

23

King Ku

MORNING came, and with it King Ku.

The boys were up and dressed and had opened the
flaps to let in the bright African sunshine. A shadow
blocked the light and they looked up from their coffee to
see a big black face.

It was Ku's face, yet it was a face they had not seen
before. This was a smiling face. It was the first time they
had ever seen the district officer smile.

'May I come in?'

'Do,' Hal said. 'Sit down. Have some coffee.'

'I don't deserve such courtesy,' said the smiling Ku,
seating himself on the edge of Hal's cot. 'I came to congratulate you on your success in taking the man-eaters.'

Hal looked at him with astonishment. 'I had a crazy
notion that you didn't want us to succeed.'

'You were right,' Ku admitted. 'Frankly, I hoped you
would have a bad accident.'

'We nearly did,' Hal said. 'When somebody cut us
adrift.'

'Who do you think could have done that?'

'We don't know. We think it may have been Dugan.
Or Basa.'

Ku's grin broadened. 'You are wrong on both counts.
I cut your line.'

'But why were you so anxious to do us in?'

'It was all a misunderstanding,' Ku said. He was not smiling now. 'You remember the Mau Mau trouble when the Kikuyus started murdering white people. Many Englishmen along with their wives and children were tortured and killed. The whites began to fight back and many Africans died at their hands. My own wife and children were murdered. I had reason to believe that whites had done this and I was possessed by a terrible hatred of any man with a white skin. So when you came along I saw my chance to take revenge. I hoped the man-eaters would get you. When they didn't, I waited for a storm to come up and then cut your line.'

Hal looked at Ku with deep sympathy. 'I don't wonder that you felt as you did after the murder of your wife and your children. But what has made you change your mind?'

'I find that I was wrong,' Ku said. 'My family was not killed by whites. The man who did the killing has confessed. He was a member of the black Mau Mau. I had refused to join the Mau Mau and take their oath to kill whites. So, to punish me, they sent this man to wipe out my family. And ever since I have been hating the wrong people for that act.'

Hal extended his hand and Ku took it. 'It doesn't matter now,' Hal said. 'After all, your cutting us adrift gave us quite a thrilling adventure. And I'm relieved to know that Basa didn't do it. Is he really going to go ahead with the school?'

'He is, and we'll help him all we can.'

King Ku had no sooner gone than the boys had two other visitors – Warden Mark Crosby and a man whom he introduced as Dr John Teller, director of the Bronx Zoo.

'Dr Teller has been staying with us at Kitani. He is interested in your Black Mane and the cub.'

Dr Teller shook hands warmly with Hal and then turned to Roger.

'So this is the boy who took a man-eater single-handed. What a story! And what a magnificent lion! I've been anxious to get to you before any other zoo director makes contact with you. Ordinarily we don't pay much for a lion – but this is a very special case. I'm prepared to offer you ten thousand dollars for Black Mane and his cub – provided you, Roger, will throw in a picture of yourself without extra charge.'

'It's a more than fair offer,' Hal said.

'But forget the picture,' put in Roger.

Dr Teller said slyly, 'Very well, forget the picture. Without the picture it'll be one thousand.'

Roger stared. 'Nine thousand dollars for a picture? What's the idea?'

'Don't you see? Without your picture and your story, this is just a lion. But, with them, it's a feature that will bring tens of thousands of people to the zoo to see a real live man-eater that was captured with kindness by a thirteen-year-old boy. It will be the main attraction of the zoo. So I advise you, young man, to swallow your modesty, and let us run your picture and story in the papers and on a marker that we will post wherever Black Mane is exhibited. Is it a deal?'

Roger objected, 'But you must keep Black Mane and the cub together.'

'Naturally. The cub is just as important as its father.

If it hadn't been for your care of the cub you wouldn't have won over Black Mane and there'd be no story. In fact, I'll put in another five thousand for the cub.'

Hal laughed. 'Let me hasten to accept your offer before you up your price any further. Usually I wire my Dad before selling. But in this case I know he'd only scold us for charging you too much.'

'Don't fool yourself,' smiled the director. 'This is not charity. I'm getting my money's worth.'

Hal turned to Crosby. 'Sorry we bunged up your balloon.'

'Don't worry about it. It's been found and we're sending a Power-wagon to pick it up. When it comes,' he added with a twinkle in his eye, 'perhaps you'd like to take another trip in it?'

'No, thanks,' said Hal.

POST A LITTLE HAPPINESS

Post·A·Book

A Royal Mail service in association with the Book Marketing Council & The Booksellers Association.
Post-A-Book is a Post Office trademark.

These are other Knight Books

Willard Price 'Adventure' stories are all about
Hal and Roger and their amazing adventures in
search of wild animals for the world's zoos.
Here is a complete list of the adventures
available in Knight:

1 AMAZON ADVENTURE
2 SOUTH SEA ADVENTURE
3 UNDERWATER ADVENTURE
4 VOLCANO ADVENTURE
5 WHALE ADVENTURE
6 AFRICAN ADVENTURE
7 ELEPHANT ADVENTURE
8 SAFARI ADVENTURE
9 LION ADVENTURE
10 GORILLA ADVENTURE
11 DIVING ADVENTURE
12 CANNIBAL ADVENTURE
13 TIGER ADVENTURE
14 ARCTIC ADVENTURE

WALTER FARLEY

The world-famous series about the Black Stallion and Alec Ramsay

All these books are available at your local bookshop or newsagent, or can be ordered direct from the publisher. Just tick the titles you want and fill in the form below.

Prices and availability subject to change without notice.

KNIGHT BOOKS, P.O. Box 11, Falmouth, Cornwall.

Please send cheque or postal order, and allow the following for postage and packing:

U.K. – 45p for one book, plus 20p for the second book, and 14p for each additional book ordered up to a £1.63 maximum.

B.F.P.O. and EIRE – 45p for the first book, plus 20p for the second book, and 14p per copy for the next 7 books, 8p per book thereafter.

OTHER OVERSEAS CUSTOMERS – 75p for the first book, plus 21p per copy for each additional book.

Name ....

Address ....

....